For C
With love & trust

MSU Denver, Feb 2019

KD

Living on happiness

MINH HAI

Living on happiness

A guide to practicing mindfulness in daily life

BODHI
MEDIA
COMPASSION PEACE MINDFULNESS

Copyright @ 2018 by Minh Hai
All rights reserved
ISBN-13: 978-1724278203
ISBN-10: 1724278207

Acknowledgement

I would like to thank Diane Nguyen, Minh Ha Kasenurm, Hoa Nguyen, Nguyen Phuc, and Ray Horn (Hanh Tri) for reading early drafts of my manuscript and giving me their valuable insight and encouragement. I am grateful to Amy Nguyen and Lynn Berggren for their deep commitment to excellence and their help on reviewing the final draft. My deep appreciation to them all, their insights and loving-kindness is what helped fueled the many hours of work necessary to bring this book to completion.

CONTENTS

ACKNOWLEDGEMENT I
INTRODUCTION V
PREFACE IX
1. Living on happiness 1
2. Walking in the footsteps of the buddha 11
3. Far away from wicked people 26
4. The great beings 33
5. Respect those who are worth honoring 39
6. Living in the good environment 44
7. Being creating good seeds 54
8. Guiding our mind toward the righteous path 60
9. Profound knowledge 67
10. Right professions 85
11. Practicing ethics 88
12. Loving speech 95
13. Filial care to parents 100
14. Raising children 105

III
CONTENTS

15. Spousal love and care 116
16. To complete duties 126
17. Giving with love 130
18. Living by the buddha's teaching 137
19. Helping relatives 141
20. Action without defect 145
21. Fear and avoid bad things 150
22. Nourishment and healing 154
23. Diligently do good deeds 160
24. Homage is beautiful 166
25. Practicing to be humble 172
26. Knowing enough is peacefull 176
27. Happiness is gratefulness 181
28. Studying buddha's teaching 192
29. Practicing patience 197
30. The shame of mistakes 206
31. Joining with spiritual life 212
32. Attending dharma sharing 215
33. Life is a miracle 220
34. Mindfulness is the purpose of life 230
35. Understanding mysterious truth 236
36. Realization of nibbana 241
37. Peace is every step 250

IV
Living on happiness

38. Calm and joyful mind 257
39. Remove affliction 263
40. Touching of life 269
41. Happiness in the present moment 274
Discourse on happiness 279
Endnotes 282

Introduction

On behalf of the team at Bodhi Media Publisher, we are pleased to present to our readers, *Living on Happiness* by Vung Q Doan aka Minh Hai. Vung Doan is a translator, mindfulness practitioner, and currently a master student studying educational psychology. He is working to bring mindfulness meditation into the field of education and to everyone at home.

Living on Happiness delivers the great message from the Buddha's teachings and teaches us how to live in a manner that brings us true happiness in life. It is an art of living according to the teachings in the *Discourse on Happiness*. The book uses light language and real life experiences to explain the Buddha's teaching, while demonstrating the bridge between Buddhist and Western psychology. This book is beneficial to us all to learn and practice how to bring happiness and peace into our lives.

Life is a miraculous gift and all of us are capable in achieving peace and happiness. However, we sometimes

VI
Living on happiness

forget or do not even realize that we are happy, because our mind is roaming in a state of illusion. An old proverb says, "when our mind lost mindfulness, the eyes look at things but we do not see, though the ears hear sound but do not know; the mouth is eating but does not know the taste of food." The goal in the practice of the Buddha's teachings is to invite the mind to return to the body, so that we can feel more meaning in life and find happiness. Mindful awareness is the key to happiness, peace, and harmony in life. Here, we realize that there is no path to happiness, happiness is the path.

The opening chapter one, the author introduced to us that happiness is the way.

> "Where to find happiness
> Abstraction or illusion
> Bright and pure mind
> Happiness is around us" (p.10).

We all have the right to aspire to a bright future or to a successful career, but every step we take on that path must be fun and joyful. Peace is a step by step process and happiness is in the present moment; these two points are important teachings in Buddhist literature. The purpose of learning and practicing the Buddha's teachings is so we have freshness, relaxation, and happiness in life.

The wisdom of Buddhism emphasizes the five basic elements to achieve true happiness. These five elements are known as the five powers; those are power of faith, power of energy, power of mindfulness, power of concentration, and power of insight. The author sequentially explains each Buddha's teaching in a concrete way and exposes it under the light of science to help readers have a better understanding of the doctrines of the Buddha in a clear, coherent and bright manner.

Happiness is very simple, if we have mindful awareness to perceive things around us. As in chapter 27, *happiness is gratitude*. Just thinking of gratitude and thankfulness can give us happiness. "*When humanity engages in behavior to build social relationships, establish peace and happiness for the families and international communities, it is called moral behavior. The content of true morals is the true love of living and gratitude... and that is the root of all virtues*" (p.182).

In the last chapter, *happiness in the present*, the author defines with the verse.

"*While facing adversity,
you can recognize your body and mind,
can stay with peace,
and find happiness in the present moment*" (p.278).

Each chapter contains a lesson for us to contemplate. This is happiness, when we know how to *create good seeds, guide our mind toward the righteous path, practice ethics, have loving speech, and give with love...* practicing and leading our lives with the followings, as taught in the *Living on Happiness*, we will no longer see suffering, feel hatred, and experience discrimination. In other words, there will be a healthier environment, a more peaceful society and a community of compassionate people. Most important of all, each person will live in happiness, peace and leisure.

Words can only describe the experience so much, the ancients said, only when you drink water yourself then you would know the water is hot or cold. Well, we invite readers to read to enjoy and experience happiness when reading this book.

We are proud to introduce the work of *Living on Happiness* with all the joy and respect. May all beings be happy and peaceful; stay safe and serene; be healthy and prosperous; and live happily and peacefully.

The Bodhi Media Publisher
Sacramento, California
July 04, 2018

Preface

Can we find happiness in this life? How can we make happiness stay with us? How about when we have troubles in our day? An angry housemate or a family member accidentally spoils our peaceful day. Unless we are robots, our minds will be shaken by these adversities. However, being happy depends on whether we are able to see the causes of our troubles and stay focused on the important goals of our lives. I realized the noble truth from my friend, an ordinary person, who is very simple but warm-hearted, kind and happy. One afternoon, when we were driving around the city of Chicago, another car suddenly crashed in front of us. Luckily, there was no accident, but the driver of the other car poked his head out the window and said impolite things. I was partially panicking when the incident occurred. However, my friend was very calm and he only smiled and greeted the other driver with the holy gesture. I asked, "How are you so kind to him? That person nearly injured us." The friend replied, "There are many people whose hearts are filled with tension, resentment, and suffering. Because of this lack of mindfulness, they are therefore full of rubbish. When they try to push their garbage on others, never react to it. Smile for our comfort and focus on our work." My friend added, "I have this calmness thanks to practicing mindfulness meditation, as taught in 'Discourse on Happiness.'[1] It teaches me to change my mind and my life, to let go of all my troubles, to feel serenity."

My friend's response encouraged me to share this path to peacefulness and happiness, in the form of the guide, *Living on Happiness*. *Living on Happiness* is derived from the initial thoughts: "Do I really live in peace and happiness? How do I react when faced with difficulties or adversities? When I am angry or suffering, do I spread that to people around me?" I tell myself not to foster this type of mentality, as I also do not want to cause hurt or pain to others. With such awareness, I try to practice living in happiness every day, so I can make positive changes and encourage more joy and happiness in the world.

To write this book, I am inspired by how many people strive to be awakened and to feel alive, to learn to overcome difficulties when facing life's challenges and sufferings. I would like to see all of you happy in every single breath and step that you take in your journey through life. Cherish what we have, because life is too short for not paying attention. I hope we all work together to build a world of peace, understanding and goodness. This book is dedicated for those who want to have a truly peaceful and happy life.

Minh Hai
University of Denver, Colorado
January 1, 2018

1

LIVING ON HAPPINESS

"Happiness does not depend on external factors but it depends on how we feel in every moment, and how we live our lives."

Suffering is a part of human life. Everybody faces the following common problems: we suffer from being apart from a loved one, dealing with disagreeable people every day, having uncompromising desires, and experiencing frustration from many other sources. These problems drain our energy and give us headaches, fatigue, and tension. However, life also gives us miracles a dream to pursue, someone who loves us wholeheartedly, a great view of a sunset from the top of a mountain, autumn leaves, or white winter snow.

Happiness and suffering always co-exist. They are interdependent: "When this exists, that comes to be; with the arising of this, that arises. When this does not exist,

Living on happiness

that does not come to be; with the cessation of this, that ceases."[2] This principle is a profound teaching in Buddhism. Suffering and happiness are two sides of life, we cannot separate them. Likewise, we cannot seek happiness from others, but only from ourselves, because happiness cannot exist without suffering. If someone brings you happiness, it is only temporary.

Everybody searches for happiness, but does anyone know the true meaning of happiness? How to make happiness? Sometimes, the more we pursue happiness, the further we have to go to achieve it. Sometimes, though, just being aware of what we have, fills us with happiness. Therefore, happiness is real, and it is right beside us, around us, and even inside us. In other words, with a mindful awareness, we could awaken the source of happiness that life has given.

Happiness sometimes is defined as the feeling of pleasure. When one is satisfied with something, that satisfaction brings him comfort. However, this does not mean that pleasure exists when the conditions for happiness exist. Consider a child, playing in front of his home, who has nothing to worry about. He is cared for and loved by his parents. Does he know that he is blessed? Many of us have many favorable conditions in life but we do not realize it, so we are not happy. Thus, the definition of happiness is the sense of being happy and enjoying what we have. Like the aforementioned child, he does not know how happy he is until he grows up or the favorable conditions are no longer available.

The idea of happiness can be thought of as us enjoying ourselves. Sometimes we work hard, but we are happy because we work for our loved ones, benefitting others and society. For example, there are volunteers who are not afraid of going to warzones to rescue victims of bombings. They have joy and happiness because they have the will of great compassion. Thus, the concept of happiness is the consciousness of all things that are happening around us right here and now.

Consider this proverb: "There is no way to happiness; happiness is the way." Happiness is often considered an ultimate goal that people seek to reach. They mistakenly believe it is the end of a journey, or a destination. Instead, happiness is an endless path. The key to happiness is not a destination of a long path, but is every step on that path. In other words, happiness does not depend on external factors but it depends on how we feel in every moment, and how we live our lives.

Additionally, happiness is a work in progress in everyday life. People falsely believe happiness is money, fame, and power, and spend all their time searching for these things, when in reality, they are often very miserable. They suffer because of competition with others who want the same power. Their concept of power is something inauthentic, hard to reach, and can only be grasped by the exclusion of others. Many people have this type of power and fame but are still suffering. Siddhattha, the precursor of the Buddha, saw the despair of a powerful and reputable ruler in his father, Suddhodana, who helplessly witnessed the injustice of contemporary society, class division, discrimination, and corruption. The concept of power in Buddhism is different. Buddha advised us that happiness must be built on healthy, non-violent relationships, and cannot cause suffering to others.

If we let go of anxiety, fear, anger, and jealousy and instead channel the energy of love, tolerance, forgiveness, and generosity, then happiness will be more permanent. The nature of power and fame is not a sin, but when we let it turn us towards worry, possessiveness, and selfishness, we become its victim. As long as our mind is dominated by anger, possessions, and the desire to have authority over others, we will not achieve happiness. People mistakenly think that we have to wait until we reach a certain position, or travel to the world of bliss and paradise, or get rid of others we hate to experience happiness. In fact, true happiness exists when we have a large, compassionate heart, and the ability to be aware of what is happening in the present situation.

Meditation helps us to gain mindful awareness, which helps us to interact with life right now and right here and makes us unconditionally happy. Happiness is not only an end goal, but something we can potentially experience through the journey as we seek it. We are only happy when we understand the lives of others living around us. We should never seek happiness by destroying what people have, such as their dreams, love, or power. Instead, we make happiness by rebuilding what has been or is failing and connecting people together.

While we enjoy and pursue money, fame, lust, overindulgence in food and sleep, Buddha called it misery, because the more desperate we are for those vices, the more we suffer. Buddha referred to the five factors that lead to happiness, called "the five powers," including the powers of faith, energy, mindfulness, concentration, and insight. These are the basis of true happiness.

The first power is *the power of faith*. It is the source of energy that comes from within, when we trust in our own ability. We have a compassionate, understanding heart and noble qualities. Tathagata, another of Buddha's titles, said that within the depths of our minds there is a hidden seed of the Buddha. Believing in the catechesis of the Buddha makes us capable of destroying suffering, attaining perfection, liberation, and enlightenment. Zen masters often advised,—"Believing in your abilities through the training of the mind, practicing to end the afflictions, and the possibility of reaching Buddhahood is enlightenment." Having faith in Dharma to open up wisdom, believing in the practice of the truth in daily life and believing in the fruitful result, is the way to be free of suffering, to achieve real happiness. The Buddha affirmed, "The holy disciples, who believe in their capability to become Buddha, have power of faith."³ If we truly believe in that doctrine and walk on this path with persistence, happiness will be with us. We will be happy with the pure belief that we can achieve compassion, wisdom, and mindfulness. In fact, if we practice well, it will bring us happiness and peace.

The second power is *the power of diligence*. We must make efforts to practice compassion and wisdom every moment to create happiness for others and ourselves. These practices are as necessary to our healthy minds as nutritious food is to our bodies. Buddha taught: "The holy disciples diligently eliminate evil and make good deeds. They are said to have the power of diligence."⁴ It is important to emphasize that we try to practice compassion and wisdom everyday, maintaining mindfulness in our lives without boasting or calling attention to what we are doing. We are merely being interesting, fun, and useful for ourselves. There are four diligent practices that are emphasized in Buddhist doctrines:

1. We must be aware of what happens in our minds and avoid any negative emotions and unwholesome thinking

2. When negative emotions or unwholesome thinking arise in the mind, we must be aware and stop them before they become actions

3. We must always regard benevolent deeds highly and encourage our minds to think about good deeds

4. *When benevolent deeds arise in the mind, support them and bring them into actions*[5]

We need to clearly see negative emotions so that diligence prevents them from arising and, instead, arouses good deeds to bring peace and happiness. By practicing diligence, we can foster a high quality of life and transform suffering into positive actions, thereby helping ourselves and others to live in peace and happiness.

The third power is *the power of mindfulness.* Mindfulness is a very essential factor in daily life. It is the energy that helps us to realize what is happening around us. The power of mindfulness helps us to have a fulfilling life every moment, to understand what is worth pursuing and what to avoid. Mindfulness shines light on our daily activities and embraces suffering, pain, or despair. Without mindfulness we live in chaos. Not knowing the proper behaviors in various situations torments ourselves and others. Buddha taught: "The holy mindful disciples, who realized wisdom, the victory of the self, and long-term practice of diligence, achieved the power of mindfulness"[6] Many people live their lives worrying about things that happened in the past or worrying about illusions of the future. They do not live their lives meaningfully. Thus, mindfulness is the energy of nourishment and healing. It is the key to true happiness.

The fourth power is *the power of concentration,* means positive? focus on the thing we are doing. For example, when eating breakfast, we should only enjoy the taste of apples, oatmeal, and cereal, and refrain from thinking with feelings of anger, despair or hatred. This concentration is important for the health of the body and mind. Buddha taught: "The holy disciples who renounce emotions gain concentration. They have power of concentration."[6] We must eliminate the delusions and/or distractions that block us from truly seeing the nature of things in a profound way. We cannot see the true beauty of a flower with a brief glance, but must use energy to appreciate the true essence of a flower. Sometimes, we face difficulties or sorrows; we need the energy of our own mind to determine the causes of those obstacles. Once we know the causes, we can easily disentangle ourselves from the pain and gain peace of mind.

The fifth power is *the power of insight*. Wisdom is like the sword used to cut off defilements. The light of wisdom helps us to see the nature of things as impermanent, not of the self, and interdependent. One of the reasons people suffer is because they think everything is permanent. They are not prepared when something is lost, and they feel grief when losing it. In reality, we do not have an independent entity called self, because everything depends on each other and we coexist with everything in this world. The perception of selflessness will show that our joy is also the joy of our family and that of the social community, and when we are sad it affects those around us. The wisdom of interdependence will give us insight into the intimate relationship between humans and all things in the universe. If we bring love to someone, we will get joy. On the contrary, causing suffering to others will bring us pain and sorrow. Buddha also taught: "The holy disciples who have wisdom; who have the intellectual mastery of the impermanence law; who apply the wisdom of the enlightened beings and thus limit suffering... They have power of insight."[7] Wisdom is the source of miraculous light that helps us to identify the essence of all living things, escape fear and intolerance and receive love, acceptance, forgiveness and tolerance. Therefore, wisdom is also the source of happiness.

These five factors build a solid foundation for a happy life. They are keys for our long-lasting happiness. The practices in this booklet were taught by Buddha. They are the steps we need to cultivate in our consciousness with faith to discover the bodhi seed within ourselves. It is necessary to distinguish between pleasure and inner peace. The nature of pleasure is craving and it can satisfy the temporary desire, but does not last long. While peacefulness is developed from the inside through practice and awareness, and peacefulness gives you a peaceful and liberating life.

The pursuit of pleasure and happiness to satisfy our craving is fragile. It is difficult to satisfy the craving. Many people end up exhausted or must suffer remorse throughout their lives. Instead, people who seek inner peace or true happiness release themselves from craving.

As they build up great compassion, sharing and living for others, happiness grows stronger. Inner peace can also be achieved through meditation, and when the mind is clear, true liberation is achieved.

The following chapters will introduce the methods to achieve happiness and inner peace, including practicing mindfulness and experiencing peace in every footstep to transform our mind and body. These methods were experienced and taught by Buddha. They have been passed on to many generations of Buddha's disciples. These methods bring great value to anyone who has the opportunity to accept and practice. They can quickly end suffering. To live in the Dharma is to live a happy life.

> *"Where to find happiness*
> *Abstraction or illusion*
> *Bright and pure mind*
> *Happiness is around us"*

2

WALKING IN THE FOOTSTEPS OF THE BUDDHA

"There is one person who arises in the world for the welfare of many people, for the happiness of many people, out of compassion for the world, for the good, welfare, and happiness of devas and human beings."

Each person has a different view of the Buddha. When you first learn about Buddhism, your opinion is different from those who have learned and practiced the Buddha's teachings for a long time. Your knowledge and understanding of the Buddha will change if you have the opportunity to practice every day, and at some point you will find that Buddhism is very close to human life. The monks said that Buddha's teachings lie in the world, so leaving the world to find the Buddha's teachings does not help one find them. When you first come into contact with the Buddha through scriptures, the perception of Buddhism is not really true, so you must be willing to let go of that notion. Then, you have the opportunity to gain new knowledge. Many people know the Buddha through written theories, and through that reading each person forms an idea of the Buddha himself. It is easy to understand once you realize that the teaching of impermanence is true. The doctrine of impermanence tells you that all phenomena never disappear but that they are manifested in another form, which means that after death they are continued but in a different way. For example, it may be foggy in the morning, but by noon with the shining sun, there is no more fog. You cannot say that the fog has died; it is manifested in a new form (steam). So, finding the Buddha is your responsibility. Where is the Buddha? Whether the Buddha is inside you or is an external entity is a concept that needs to be raised for discussion.

I remember the first day of visiting the monastery, seeing fruits and flowers presented on the Buddha's shrine by the monks on a weekly basis. I thought that Buddha used fruit! During the morning meditation, I was always staring at the fruit plate to see if the Buddha had grasped a grapefruit, orange, or apple. Seeing that the fruit plate remained the same after a few days, I told myself that Buddha was embarrassed because I always watched the plate. Thus, he refused to eat. That afternoon, after the meditation, with the Buddha's door closed, the lights out, and nobody in the meditation hall, I decided to stay behind the door to observe. Maybe the Buddha would take the fruit when there were no monks and followers sitting in the hall. Waiting and waiting, as I looked at a statue of the Buddha, I still saw nothing but the Buddha sitting quietly and smiling.

When you research the history of Shakyamuni Buddha and read all the sutras, you learn that Crown Prince Siddhattha was born in Kapilavatthu, was well educated, handsome, and grew up in a palace of emeralds and velvet silk - a life of privilege and luxury that could afford him to live the rest of his life in comfort and ease. However, Siddhattha took a different course in adulthood... he left home to attend the monastery. He lived six years of asceticism, sat under the Bodhi tree to attain enlightenment, traveled throughout the Ganges basin for 45 years, and then died when he was 80 years old. When Buddhists draw his image, it is the image of Shakyamuni based on that information. The Buddha's image was like that, but after his passing, the image of the Buddha became different. Therefore, you must study deeply to avoid being trapped in the image of the Buddha that you know through the sources of literature.

Like many other religions in this world, when you come to Buddhism you also need an image of the teacher to take refuge in that practice, which is Buddha Shakyamuni. A difference, though, is that you have to understand his doctrine so as not to get caught up in that image. If you think that the old Buddha is as it is now, that is a big mistake. If you think that the Buddha is still somewhere in space or living in some pure land after entering nibbana, then you are in an obstinate state. Buddhists call this the *doctrine of immortality*. If you think that the Buddha is gone and no longer exists, then another attachment is called *annihilation-illusion*. Both are not quite right. Therefore, when you embrace Buddhism you need to practice how to contact the Buddha, to truly see him rather than simply conceptualize him. If you fall into the state of doctrine of immortality or annihilation-illusion, then you will be unable to find Buddha. When you first come into contact with Buddhism, you rely on the image of the Buddha through the sources of sutras, but then you go further to see that the image is also impermanent. It means that the Buddha is followed by a different form, which is very clear.

We must dismiss the mythical admiration and respect for the Buddha, made by many generations of his disciples who have ceaselessly embellished and solemnly extolled him as a legendary figure. All of that reverence comes from the respect and deep gratitude of what Buddha has contributed to humanity. Buddha said that what enlightenment he attained came completely free from the efforts and wisdom of men, as human beings are only able to understand the heart of human aspirations. Only human beings have the ability to become a Buddha, and the spirits cannot understand human psychology. We all have the ability to become Buddha if we can carry great diligence to practice the Buddha's teachings. Thus, from the

Buddhist point of view, human beings have self-control, so there is no higher entity or power that can determine their fate. The Buddha taught himself to be a refuge himself; no one else could be his refuge.

The advancement of present science has shown that cells in the body die every second. The human mind also changes in every moment, and if you think deeply, you can see that the lines of thought, speech, and action are constantly changing. These actions bring your mark through the daily life of the three activities which thought, speech and acttion. The resulting actions of the three activities are stored and followed in a precise and specific way. This shows you the continuity of the Buddha through the thought taught to his disciples.

How to adapt to each culture, according to the level of each person, is called the right thinking. When you know to enjoy beauty, or want to learn to be good, you are a person who is on the path of wisdom. See the right view to fit into each territory, community, culture of each country, and human tradition. The Buddha was a human being who symbolized wisdom; this wisdom is a transparent understanding, always adapted to each person through each historical event. Reading Buddhist scriptures, you will see clearly the combination of science and talent of the Buddha who put his doctrine to the people.

There are many levels of catechism of Buddha's teaching, but I would like to tell you that in letting

Buddhism return to its pristine nature, you see that it is a living art, a path of moral and spiritual education. The Zen masters often teach the new yogis that when praying before Buddha, to visualize that you and the Buddha are two realities, but not separated. You see clearly the Buddha is inside you and you also in him, because Buddha and his students are inter-being. Therefore, the sympathy of the Buddha and you becomes very close and deep. It is a practice of visualizing before bowing to the Buddha to see that you can touch the Buddha himself, not just his thoughts.

Many generations of Buddhists have been dedicated to promoting the teachings of the Holiness so that others can perceive and understand how these can be applied to life. The Buddha's teachings are capable of transforming the inherent suffering of life into peacefulness and happiness. Although the individual Buddhist disciplines are slightly different in terms of their practice, they all have the same purpose: to lead people to overcome suffering, to find peace and happiness in life. Buddhist scholars have agreed that Buddhism is a pathway to human good in solving the urgent and important problems of life, especially the suffering of human beings. This was also the ambition of the Buddha, who said: "One person, my disciples, with his existence in life, brings happiness to the majority, peace for the majority, for the sake of life, for the benefit, for the happiness, and for the peace of gods and humans. Who is that one person? It is the world Lord, the Buddha."

Dealing with suffering and bringing peace to people is the essence of Buddhism. You will not find anything other than that message in the treasury of the sutras. The Anglo-German scholar and lecturer, Edouard Conze, talked about Buddhism as an entity that brought people back to the present to solve the difficulties of life. Suffering is a big problem in human life; you cannot run away from it, nor deny it with vague knowledge that lacks wisdom and understanding.

Mahayana missionaries brought Buddhism into life with the beautifully illustrated images of the Buddha's majestic enlightened wisdom. The Bodhisattvas, such as *Avalokiteshvara, Manjushri, Samantabhadra, Kshitigarbha,* and *Sadaparibhuta,* often expressed the very clear wish to free human beings from suffering in darkness and bring their teachings of liberation to humanity. These were very lively and creative images of the senior forebears in the early stages of Buddhist history. These images have become so sacred and alien to human beings that people often like to paint their images with beautiful details, adding pearls and jewelry to their heads and shoulders. Of course, to worship the holy lords we should personify their form and beautify them. In actuality, these Bodhisattvas are the simplest and the poorest people in life; they have loving hearts without boundaries, and their compassion for human beings is tireless and unlimited.

The true image of Bodhisattva *Avalokiteshvara* symbolizes listening to the suffering of the world; hearing with a compassionate heart without discrimination; hearing without condemnation, judgment, or reproach; hearing to find understanding; and helping others to reduce their suffering.

The image of the Bodhisattva *Manjushri* is symbolic of knowing to pause and gaze deeply into the heart with attention, to have the crucial understanding of the root of all difficulties and obstacles in life, and then use the sword to cleave the bind.

Understanding Bodhisattva *Samantabhadra*, people know to bring their eyes and hearts to life, to offer joy, to bring cheer to everyone. He is always aware that the happiness of others is his own happiness.

Think of the Bodhisattva *Kshitigarbha* as living in the dark to bring ease, soothing the people who make mistakes. Imagine a person who cares for patients who are trapped in beds. Such a bodhisattva never abandons nor ignores those who are trapped in lonely despair, who have no means of escape or no means to call for justice, right to freedom, and equality.

The image of Bodhisattva *Sadaparibhuta* is of one who finds the secret treasure trove in every one of us. He gladly announces to dying people that they should not be afraid, but that they should open the treasure within instead. The message from this Bodhisattva is "I dare not despise you, because you will become a Buddha." There are many people who do not accept this, so they scold or beat him, but he is not discouraged or turned to shame.

The images of these Bodhisattvas have great humanitarian values and are majestic, wonderful expressions of the liberating nature of Buddhism. However, humans have forgotten the true or depth of beauty, and worship only as if to prostrate before a god and pray. It is regrettable if you cannot touch the depths of this mystery. The image must be in your heart for your soul to become simple, pure, and beautiful. When these images always reign in your heart, you will be shaken by the infinite compassion for all people and things. You arise to the desire to share, sympathize, and sacrifice.

The image of the Buddha represents a simple way of life. It transmits the teachings of liberation for people to transform the mind rather than to worship. The mission of the Bodhisattvas is to bring the message of enlightenment into the world, to help people to escape suffering and live in peace and happiness. Many generations have carried the message and the nature of Buddhism in a very successful way. However, we should refrain from painting those bodhisattvas in accordance to our own thinking, as it will spoil the original teaching of Buddha. The spreading of popular beliefs distorts the dynamic image of Buddhism. Some people are turning the Buddha into a distant divinity frozen in the expression of praying. Humans need to worship, but it is more important to understand the form of worship and the meaning of worship.

20
Living on happiness

Understanding the teaching of Buddha deeply, means that you understand the true meaning of Buddhism. Buddha was born to reconstruct what had fallen, rebuild forgotten moral values, and bring the light of wisdom to shine in the dark. The Buddha discovered that true happiness is enlightened by love, compassion, and wisdom. The light of insight helps us understand the function of the human mind, life, and the universe. Thanks to this wisdom, we know how to love ourselves and give love to others. Therefore, when we come to the Buddha, we must ask him to teach us the practice of transforming the mind, bringing forth the source of wisdom, love, and kindness; not to beg for a miracle from him. Buddha is a true human being with a body just like all human beings in the world, so we should not expect him to perform any miracle to make us free from grief by pleading or praying. It can be affirmed that if any Buddhist tradition proclaims the Buddha to be a saving deity who can give relief to sentient beings, it is a superstitious religion and not true Buddhism.

The great happiness we experience when we come to the Buddha is absolute peace and holiness. It shows us that the Buddha is a living person who is aware of mindfulness, compassion, wisdom; escaping the bond of life to reach his own shore. You can enjoy this happiness by practicing, not by praying for liberation, happiness, or freedom. We do not ask the shore to come to us so that we may step forward. If we want to step upon the shore of peace, leisure, and freedom, then we have to use a boat or raft and row it ashore. That is the Buddha's teachings.

Because of his emphasis on peace and holiness, the Buddha provides a great resource for human happiness. He was the embodiment of enduring virtue, compassion, and serving for all beings. He led an exemplary life, teaching love, peace, and a direction for human fate. His achievements show that Buddha was a most admirable teacher. The Buddha was a person, capable of giving almost mystical teachings so that we can practice peace and happiness in this present life. Not only humans, but also the heavenly beings, bowed to him. In the opening of the *Discourse on Happiness*,[7] the goddess in the verse asked Buddha: "Many gods and men are eager to know what the greatest blessings are that bring about a peaceful and happy life. Please, Lord Buddha, will you teach us?"[8]

Why is there human suffering? Why does the world still have hatred; Because people lack compassion. They have attachments and entangled minds. Compassion helps people to overcome all ideological barriers, to create a world of harmony, peace, and happiness. Buddha taught that human success and happiness cannot be compensated by the struggles or failures of others. Why is our happiness based on the suffering of others? Why is our success based on another's failure? When we succeed, others can also succeed, so our happiness will be greater and more complete because no one will hurt or suffer from our success. True happiness is when people have hearts of love and understanding. When people have love, then there is no concept of mutual exclusion.

Many people have the ability to let go, so they have peace, joy, and happiness in life. Conversely, when we are confined in anxiety, or sadness, there is not much happiness. Some people wake up with a smile and are happy to drive to work because they love their job. They see life is worth living. There are other people who miserably drive to work every morning. When at work, they only think of the time to leave, as they are not fond of the day that lies ahead of them. Buddha taught that happiness is when one sees the cause of suffering, but never runs away from it in order to find happiness. Because the nature of life is suffering, there is more disappointment than peace and harmony.

Buddhism can contribute to the moral values of today's society because the Buddha's practices transform the body and mind in order to attain awakening. Peace is achieved through the practice of his teachings that are beyond the standard material happiness of the people that are inherent in the top of their career; the happiness that the material facilities cannot bring. It is no coincidence that Albert Einstein said: "The religion of the future will be a cosmic religion. It should transcend a personal God and avoid dogmas and theology. Covering both the natural and the spiritual, it should be based on a religious sense arising from the experience of all things, natural and spiritual, as a meaningful unity. Buddhism answers this description."[9] However, we will be far away and never touch the true value of Buddhism if we do not understand it in terms of knowledge and practice, applying the teachings to life, family, society, education as a cure for the body and a mental transformation.

The five areas of mindfulness training include the protection of life, true happiness, true love, listening and loving speech, nourishment and healing,[10] which are precious gems that establish moral standards for individuals, families, and communities. The area of listening and loving speech include concepts such as the re-establishment of communication, the resolution of the internal conflict, and the conflicts between children, spouses, and co-workers are part of the Noble Eightfold Path that can help to resolve difficulties in today's society. Mindfulness is the key not only for returning to our own contact with the miraculous life through the method of mindfulness breathing, but it is also the practice that helps us identify suffering in our stressful lives. This teaching is well suited to practical application in contemporary life, especially for the people living in today's busy society.

The four noble truths in life are based on the principle that the cause of suffering is due to ambition, hatred, and desire that cannot be achieved, which leads to depression. There is hope that as long as you look deeply into your mind, accept what you have and are happy with it, you will find happiness. There are problems in life that people have to face whether they are good people or spoiled children; inexperienced spouses, difficulties at work, illness, unhappiness, etc. No matter how much money or knowledge we have, we cannot solve the problems of suffering and despair. There was a doctor who specialized in anesthesia and was a very talented, successful and wealthy American. Unfortunately, he committed suicide in his luxurious mansion where he and his wife had lived together for a long time. He confessed that he loved a private secretary in his office, although he was married with two children. His death was a consequence of his despair and depression when he lost his mistress, as she followed another young man. The story shows us that the doctor with a high position in society still has psychological problems because of a lack of mindful practice; he still faces deadlock and chooses death as an end to despair. Through learning and practicing Buddha's teachings, we see clearly the operation of the mind; the mind is calm, not disturbed, when facing the loss or gain or praise of life.

The Buddhist's doctrine aims to find the cause of suffering and looks for the way to transform suffering into peace. The Buddha's message: "There is one person who arises in the world for the welfare of many people, for the happiness of many people, out of compassion for the world, for the good, welfare, and happiness of devas and human beings."[11] The cause of suffering is people living in ignorance. Many dharma talks are recorded in the scriptures to help us remove the ignorance, the wrong perception, and give us the ability to let go and find happiness in the present moment. Thus, the Buddha's path is not for the purpose of metaphysical reasoning, the origin of the universe, or determining for how long mankind has existed. Buddhism focuses on practical methods to meet the cause of suffering in the logical order according to the level of each person, from the lay person to the monastic, with intensive practice. The path is built on the foundation of mindfulness, wisdom through the Four Noble Truths, and the Noble Eightfold Path, along with the thirty-seven virtues that help us to heal and transform our body and mind. It has conquered millions of hearts over the course of history in the past twenty-six centuries, from kings, intellectuals, and merchants, to civilians in society.

Understanding the role of Buddhism and applying his teachings in life will bring us many valuable benefits, overcome the limits of religion, and help to transform mind and body. Changing minds will change lives. When the mind is gentle and serene, we will look at life with compassionate eyes and then peace and fun will exist.

> "Buddha has the whole beauty
> Full of mercy and wisdom
> The world is often revered
> The Teacher of the gods and men."

3

FAR AWAY FROM WICKED PEOPLE

"As a human, when we are close to friends who have the will to rise, the great heart, the holy life, then those good qualities will infect us and encourage us to succeed. Conversely, dealing with bad friends will make us put off our future, like going down a small alley without a way to get out."

If we live our lives apart from good friends, we will lack the motivation to learn, we will have no purpose to strive for, and sometimes we will be left out of society. We all live in one community, breathe the same air, and we should participate in activities together. All the people around us directly or indirectly affect our lives. They sometimes influence us positively, making us sublime, happy and peaceful, but sometimes they affect us in a negative way that can hurt us and create insecurities in our lives.

27
FAR AWAY FROM WICKED PEOPLE

Buddhist psychology says that as a newborn our mind is neither kind nor evil, a state of being called "unsigned." How a person matures is influenced by the educational environment, surrounding family and friends, and geographical circumstances; nurture over nature.

Young people especially experience a great deal of influence from their friends and surroundings. A baby is very sensitive, with the ability to absorb information and learn language or any kind of data very quickly. At this age there are more than one hundred million nerve joints, twice as many as adults.[12]

Therefore, not surprisingly, the Buddha advised us to choose good wholesome friends to be close to, to have the opportunity to learn the right things. If we are close to the unwholesome or wicked people, it will not bring peace to us and it will lead us to the dark paths of life. The personalities of the people around you are like food and nutrients for your brain, they enter your mind in a subtle way that you cannot perceive without awareness.

When it comes to the mind, there are many types of information or inputs which act like foods for the mind that have the power to nourish and heal. But if you are not strong enough, there are also types of information that can hurt and inhibit bodhicitta, the spontaneous desire to attain enlightenment through great compassion for others. You must be clever to have the right understanding to identify which foods are good for the mind and which are harmful. When you choose foods that are gentle and nutritious for the mind, you will have happiness and peace for the body and the mind.

In this way your life will be fresh and gentle. It is in being with the gentle wholesome person as you walk in the fog that you will learn the virtues. On the contrary, being close to evil people, filled with riots and hunger, will damage the body and mind, and then damage life. In the Mahāmaṅgala Sutta, the Buddha taught how to live in the way that brings joy and happiness.

The Pali word, *bāla*, in English translates as 1/ ignorance, delusion, and 2/ foolish, unreasonable, fatuity. Thus, Bāla refers to the person who is thoughtless and lacking mental acuity. A person who lives without purpose and hangs suspended in life without the will to strive. We can imagine what happens to us when we are close to these types of people. Certainly, we will be infected by unwholesome seeds, because in us there are the good seeds of love, understanding, forgiveness, and tolerance, but there are also the unwholesome seeds of violence, blame, jealousy, and anger.

Good and evil always exist in a confusing way within the human mind. When you come into contact with a good person, the good seed sprouts and blooms, and the bad seed has no chance to grow in the mind. Life is intertwined, you can be influenced by others or you can influence others. In a situation where you are close to a

FAR AWAY FROM WICKED PEOPLE

bad person who you have not been able to transform, you may be led by this person to the dark path of suffering. An old man said: "Near the ink is black, near the lamp is bright, stay in calabash is round, stay in a tube will turn long." You can imagine a group of drunks, about to commit a robbery. That energy is very bad. They have lost their reasoning because of craving, and they act blindly and with aggression. If you are in that group, you absorb that harmful energy.

Psychologists tell us that children grow up unsuccessful in life, drop out of school, and fall into the lust of sin because they are closely associated with friends who have no direction in life, no purpose to live, and easily give up when faced with difficult obstacles in their life. We will become disoriented when we are close with those who do not know how to strive, have a decayed will, and are mentally damaged. It is like a poison arrow poisoning the body and mind. Associating with bad and evil friends results in a bad name finding us, and our mind becomes sluggish, such as a traveler passing through the desert with not much food left.[13]

There was a young man who dropped out of school to look for work. But the young man had a lot of difficulty finding a job because he did not have a degree. Faced with such difficulties, the young man met me, and I learned that he had associated with uneducated peers, which interfered with his evolutionary growth. The heart full of passion was extinguished because he interacted with people who lacked any faith and spirit of life. It is lucky that he listened to my advice and decided to return to school. Now he is a senior in the electronics industry. His family is very happy and think a miracle happened. The true fact is that when he returned to school he abandoned his community of bad friends.

In life, if we are close to friends who have the will to rise up, have a great heart, and live a holy life, these good qualities will affect us and encourage us to succeed. Conversely, having bad friends will cut off your future, like getting into an alley with no way out. So, it is important to stop interacting with someone who only says but never acts, who does not respect other people's possessions, who says flattering things but who cannot modestly control their consumption. Do not take that person as a friend. Often the nature of bad people is to entice good people to do wrong. They are often happy when others suffer. These people like to do things that are not their responsibility, i.e., they interfere with others to cause frustration. The minds of these people contain unrighteousness, misery, greed, and wrong view. They speak in vain, enacting evil without shame. They not only hurt themselves, but also the people around them. Their minds enjoy harassment, which leads to misconceptions and the inability to distinguish between right and wrong. When presented with good advice, or truth, or compassion, they will not listen and will only get angry and defensive. They are very difficult to subdue and rarely follow rules, whether the rules are religious or not.

31
FAR AWAY FROM WICKED PEOPLE

Therefore, you need to be aware of exposing yourself to bad people. If you are not qualified to transform the bad people, then it is better not to be close to them. Buddha said, "If you do not find one that is better than yourself, you should rather live alone, and do not be close to the fool." Proximity to an unhealthy person not only hurts our body and mind and the honor of our ancestors but is also destructive to future generations.

Being close to a bad person is an opportunity for the mind to come into contact with unhealthy toxins and to make your mind grieve, fear, and fall into despair. Today's modern society presents a challenge to human life. Humans are deeply enthralled with the changes in science and technology, with a goal of economic profit and resulting loss of their human nature. The advancement of entertainment media in the form of television, movies, social media networks, along with the world-wide internet have created an unhealthy environment for the youth. The generation that has grown up with technology has been exposed to violent games, online platforms filled with hateful content, sexually charged media and advertisement which has drowned them in a blanket of negativity and fear. In school there is a lot of bullying, violence, stigma, and anger, and many parents do not want to send their children into that environment.

Therefore, if you want to be happy and peaceful, do not be close to bad people, and never step into the dark environment. The Buddha advised: "Avoid evil elephants, horses, bulls, dogs, snakes, avoid boulders, thorns, deep holes, mountains, ponds, puddles. There are seats that do not deserve to be sat upon, the places from which we should stay away, if we socialize with bad people then our fellow practitioner will suspect and be contemptuous; He will avoid that unworthy place, the place where you should not go with those evil friends." You have to be mindful to enlighten yourself, using right understanding to guard your body and mind. Far away from unsafe places, there is no affliction, and happiness is in the present moment.

> *"Far away from the bad influence*
> *Avoid suffering*
> *Body not binding*
> *Let go of afflictions."*

4

THE GREAT BEINGS

"The great beings can be a very ordinary person in the midst of life, without many material possessions, but he has an immeasurable loving kindness, compassion, inner joy, perfect equanimity, and has a loving heart without boundaries."

The virtue of intellectuality is an integral part of our character and lifestyle. Our parents help us become a good virtuous intellectual. A good intellectual or wise man often helps us through difficult times in life, showing us how to cultivate a virtuous, spiritual, and happy life. With such friends, your life will be stable, the future will be good over time. Good friends are always happy for us and help us succeed in life. Buddha taught that when we are close to the good virtue of knowledge, we will hear useful advice. By hearing the good things, you will have a happy life and true peace.

34
Living on happiness

From Pali, *pandita*, the English translation is 1 / wise, 2 / skillful, 3 / careful, and 4 / clever. Pandita means good knowledge, a wise man, who has great morals. Intellectuals are not just high-level learners of geographic, scientific, or conventional astronomy as we think. *Good knowledge* is defined as: "Wise people or intellectuals, are the ones who, before doing anything, would always ensure that their actions do not harm themselves and others; And their only thought would be how to benefit themselves, others, the whole society, and the world. So, you called them the wise good intellectual."[14]

Humans always have an interest in eating, clothing, and comforting materials. However, the ultimate goal is how to end suffering, to achieve true happiness and true peace. One who has solidity has a great heart of compassion by giving us a gift of more faith in life. Long-term happiness will come to those who are close to and learn from virtuous people. Learning from intellectuals helps the practitioner develop kindness and virtue. Being close to the virtuous, knowledgeable human increases belief, literature, and wisdom. So, dear friend, be close to the good knowledgeable one.

In Buddhist literature, a good person is a person who practices, speaks, and walks in a conscious way. It is a person who has a clear liberated truth. A gentle person can be a very ordinary person in the midst of life, without much material fame, but he has altruism, knows causality, and has a loving heart without boundaries. Buddha taught,

35
THE GREAT BEINGS

"The person who meditates, enjoys tranquility and avoids excitement, that is, the enlightenment, mindfulness, is who people admire and respect."[15]

The wise man always looks forward to a complete perfect truth, the desire to be transformed in mind and body, and always encourages us to do things that are beneficial for others, bringing happiness to family members, community, and society. The Buddha said, "Dear friends, how do we define who we call good friends, close friends, and true friends, and cultivate a complete way to liberation? He practices the knowledge, the right mind, right speech, right action, right effort, right mindfulness, right concentration. He distances himself from wrong view, like lust, killing, but moves forward to achieve true joy in life. So, dear friends, good friends, close friends, and true friends are described in the following way: "The guru advises us to be close to the wise, because they give you peace and nature your compassion, impregnating you with a fresh heart. Being close to a wise intellectual means you are in a good environment. There are three classes of good knowledge:"[16]

The person who is able to guide and teach us on the path of the spiritual, freeing all worries and fear, beyond all suffering, to have happiness in life, is called the teacher with virtue knowledge.

The person who walks with you on all paths, not only in happy times and successes, but even in humiliation, sadness, failure, revenge... he who always tries to stick with you like glue, he is the intellectual companion.

The person who is always willing to help you out with material and spiritual needs, especially in the face of suffering, is called an externally clear and deeply understanding friend.

It can be seen in people why they are called good people; they always do good deeds and practice moral principles in daily life. It is good human beings who always respect and protect the life of all things and all species, not causing death, but instead always having compassion for life. Violence, hatred, and ambition are transformed by the attitude of openness, non-attachment, and non-discrimination. That is the way of the wise man. When they see clearly and know their mistakes, they correct, then try diligently to not repeat those mistakes again.

If other people make mistakes, the wise intelligent human will joyfully ignore the error, not hold on to the heart. The wise mind is precious, i.e. not hiding his faults, not bragging of his good. At the same time, it protects the six bases, i.e. do not say bad things, do not expose the sins of others, and often praise the good of others. The wise man not only finds the benefits of long-term happiness in his present and the future lives; he also gives these benefits to others.

These are the good and beautiful characteristics of the wise man: "Dear friends, there are three special characteristics and specialties of the wise man. Dear friend, the wise man has the right thought, right speech, and right action. This is a wise man, a good intellectual person."[17] Being close to a person with loving kindness can nourish our will, and our idealism will not be worn out, nor be distracted.

The person living in happiness and peacefulness is a person who has a holy life, sharing joy, forgiveness, and tolerance. Thus, they are good to themselves and also can bring joy to many others. They practice joy by seeing the success of others and by sharing comfort and support when others have difficulty in life. They do not hurt another person either by word or gesture or action. By doing so, they are contributing to the creation of a secure and peaceful society.

When we associate with these wholesome people, we will naturally have peace and our mind will become lighter and more joyous. When we come to the meditation center, this is the ideal environment to develop spiritual life, where the students can practice Buddha's teachings in daily life. Every step of mindfulness, each breath, and each smile have the qualities of love and transformation. When many students meditate together, everyone is fresh, everyone is happy, letting go of worries and anxiety... this is the material of peace and joy. When you are in it, you will inherit the gentle, cool energy of the community that penetrates into your consciousness, which is called *mindfulness*.[18]

Living on happiness

Even if you are not a practicing meditator in the Buddhist tradition, when you go to the practice center, you can open your mind to receive the energy of peace. The meditators work with you to create fresh energy, and everyone inherits it. Monasteries in the Buddhist tradition often have a regular daily practice, which is an ideal environment for all refugees to develop inner life. You live in that environment, you feel secure, there is freedom, and you know the righteous way to go. This is the sign of peace and happiness in life, and the development of a spiritual life towards the liberation of nibbana. You should stay close to wise people and also live in a good environment.

> *"Close to the noble one*
> *Happiness is worth living*
> *Overcome all danger*
> *Take us to Nibbana."*

5

RESPECT THOSE WHO ARE WORTH HONORING

"An honorable person is the revered one, the highest offer is his capability of directing you to the practice that is able to help you to release suffering to achieve peacefulness and happiness."

Human life requires food to nourish the body, but at the same time you need spiritual energy to nurture and care for the spirit. Regardless of the religion, teachers are capable of directing you to practice according to the disciplines. Such teachers as Zen Masters, the Dalai Lama in Buddhism, and the papal theologians are indispensable.

The Pali word pūjā, translates into English as honor, reverence, and respect. Pūjā ca pūjanīyānam is translated as *to honor those who are worthy, to honor the respectable.* A worthy person is a person of virtue, solidity, great compassion, wisdom, and understanding of the paths that lead us to the path of holiness.

The practice of mindfulness and right understanding makes it easy to distinguish who has good qualities and who are worthy of respect. There are people who, on the outside, appear to live in luxury but are not really respectable. In life, you can meet many of these people. Of course, you should keep the attitude of respect for everyone, as this is expected in all relationships. The revered one is the person who can give you peace without fear, to help train your mind and body, which is called the giving of fearlessness, confidence, and security. Venerable masters in the Buddhist tradition are teachers of great compassion, wisdom and giving. Such people are honorable people, high in virtue by living the gentle life, fully giving to bring happiness to others and the community.

In the Sutra, one day the Buddha asked his disciples: "If anyone asks: Which teachers are worth revering, respecting, worshiping, serving, and offering? You should answer: if they see the color without getting infected, leaving greed and selfish love, abandoning lust, staying away from desire, keeping a silent static mind, avoiding illegal actions, promoting equality, doing good work and doing the same with the ears, the nose, the tongue, the body, the mind, and the dharma. Such teachers are worthy of respect, honor, worship, and offerings."[19]

41
RESPECT THOSE WHO ARE WORTH HONORING

The supreme offering of a revered one is the ability to guide us through the practice to help us escape the suffering and achieve happiness. This method helps you to understand, accept, and love yourself and truly be happy. A revered one is also able to reconcile, love, and understand others. As a being, everyone has the need to be understood and to be loved, but there are times because of our clumsiness we do not know how to be nice, so we become distressed and disappointed. That is why you need a spiritual teacher to guide you how to live in peace and freshness. Happiness comes when you are aware of what is around you and accept what you have. When your mind is no longer suffering, urgent, dissatisfied, lonely, and desperate, the Pure Land or heavenly presence is here. In life, if you have an opportunity to be close to mindfulness masters, nothing compares to this blessing.

In Buddhist literature, the Buddha also reminded us that parents are worthy of our esteem and offering, because these are the two divine beings in your life. The act of manifesting a supreme virtue of humanity and a beautiful culture of humanity in the East as well as the West is often praised. Your life has the joy of peaceful happiness. It is a wonderful gift to reward your parents and the masters who have given you the wisdom that you presently have.

Sometimes in life you encounter more dissatisfaction than satisfaction, so you always nurture mindfulness to transform the unsatisfactory. One of the inevitable parts of living is the collision with adversity. This is the up and down aspect of life. So, you need patience and tolerance as you may experience loss, but you will have peace. Negative talk and arguments of right and wrong, all just create more trouble and do not benefit spiritual development. For some people that you deeply know and have many experiences with, but cannot be close to, it is best to stay away. "Even the Buddha does not want to be involved in the class of evil, let alone us."[20] It is not that Buddha is powerless to face the bad person, but perhaps this is a practical way of teaching you to think about how to deal with bad teachers and evil friends.

Not only avoiding, Buddha also advises that there should be no relationship with the evil person. Whatever their position or status in society or even in the religion, even if they promise to help you with so many good things–... if you realize that they are evil, you should not cooperate, work, or share with these people. Instead, you need long-term refuge with the one of intellectual virtue to learn and advance in the path of spirituality to develop the dharma peace in life.

The sign of peace is present when we know how to stay away from bad people (*bāla*), because until we find peace we do not know how to distinguish good and evil and have a tendency to follow the bad. Being close to the virtuous one (*pandita*), who has a refreshed life, peace, stability, alertness, and speaks and acts as the Dharma, brings us closer to enlightenment. We give reverence offerings (*pūjā*) to the one of intellectual virtue, the one who deserves to be honored. This is a precious act that you should perform.

As the opposite of the moon and the sun, and as the distance of this side of the ocean and across the ocean, the difference between bāla and pandita is similar. In the sutras, the master gives a wonderful picture of these differences: "Dear children, first, heaven and earth are very far, far apart. Second, the coast and the other shore, are a very far distance, far apart. From the sunrise to the sunset, these are the three things that are very far, far apart. The rule of the immoral class and the Dharma of good people, are the four things very far away from each other."[21]

Happiness comes at your fingertips; just be careful to learn from and be close to a respectable spiritual teacher. The teacher's mindfulness can show you the way to go. You can ask yourself if you know the direction or not? What road are you walking on? If not, look for a spiritual teacher to learn. If you already know your way, then be happy. That is the message the Buddha sends to you!

> "Respect the honorable, those who are worth honoring
> To practice the Buddha's teaching in everyday life
> Throwing away withering thoughts, fears
> Mindfulness living peacefully."

6

LIVING IN THE GOOD ENVIRONMENT

> *"The ideal place where the Buddha would like to see you is defined as the resident living in harmony, practicing the Buddha's teaching. To living artfully in the midst of life, where there is the security, the development of spiritual life, and true peace, then you will have the Dharma joy."*

The environment has a direct and indirect effect on your life, which is a very important factor that can bring happiness to your life but can also make you feel uneasy if the environment you are in is unfavorable and violent. It is essential to choose a healthy environment for yourself. Living in an ideal, safe, educated, and loving environment will not only benefit you, your family, and your society, but will also benefit the next generation by providing them with clear direction. In contrast, being in an unhealthy environment, which is full of violence, hatred, and hunger, the children will grow up to be corrupt. This is not only about choosing the ideal environment, but about working together to establish a good environment upon which others can rely. Ideal living brings a serene substance to life when in a good environment; i.e. there is the positive essence ~~from~~ when a group of people who respect the notion of self-sustaining come together, similar to a rising spirit of a true perfect life that embraces truth, goodness, and beauty.

The Pali word *patirupadesavaso* means living in a suitable country, a safe place to live, or a healthy environment. In that environment, there is a community of peaceful, non-conflicting, harmonious people who are no longer selfish, but often help one another. Residents there do not necessarily have nice houses, magnificent villas, nor do they live in crowded metropolitan areas, but instead live where residents treat each other with sympathetic eyes, loving speech, with gestures of dignified action, and respect in the spirit of selflessness. Living in harmony in that environment is: "Having surrendered my own mind, and living only according to the mind of their venerable ones."[22] The place of residence should be one in which you have intellectual friends who have a direct and orderly life. This place is convenient for you to nurture a good heart so you can learn and become a good person for family and society.

We must recognize the importance of an ideal environment that is convenient for the development of finances for our families, good education for our children, then observe how the city has been developed; does the community in which you live have a stable economy? is your property safe? and does the environment have the social evils of narcotics and crime? Especially important, can you find the Buddha's teachings in the place where you live? Are there practicing centers to learn and develop spiritual life? If the answers to these questions are yes, then conditions are met then it is the most ideal environment.

Nowadays, social development, especially in European-American society, means most cities are building on the basis of a model in which all the comforts of human life are available, which involves the development of companies to create enterprises. There are many jobs, there are elementary schools, high schools, colleges, universities, and there are religious places of worship. However, there are many parents who have lost faith in schools because they feel their children are polluted by violence, hatred, and discrimination. Fundamentally, the educational environment is ethical for both the professor and the student, however, we have also witnessed many disasters occurring in schools, such as gun violence. The problem lies in each person's individuality; we have ideologies. There are also attractive lesson plans, but we ourselves do not practice catechism. When faced with suffering, we do not know how to handle and control ourselves.

I have had the experience of seeing a university professor teaching a law and ethics course. The doctrines taught in the course were so richly endowed by philosophers

- the famous Western philosophy as developed by Plato, Socrates, Rene Descartes, Thomas Hobbes, etc. However, when the professor faced suffering, he could not control himself, and became angry at the students. My point is to say that school is not always a good environment or an ideal place for our children.

The ideal residence that the Buddha would like to introduce to you is defined as living in harmony, practicing good deeds, or the places where human beings live with social justice, where ethical conduct is practiced, and security and equal freedom are respected.

Sometimes you cannot find the right environment for yourself for many different reasons. In this case make your own environment or island for yourself which creates a suitable or worthy country for yourself to rely on. Instead of depending on the environment, you improve the environment in which you are self-sufficient, i.e. teaching yourself self-care, not allowing yourself to be affected by the external environment, and at the same time promoting loving contentment for everyone around. If you can have trust in your own island, then there is joy and peace.

When there are many joys in life you call it the paradise of a green planet, and when your mind is bored you called it the realm of "grandma talk." Whenever we encounter uncertainties, we do not have the energy of inner consciousness to contemplate the root cause, but we always have the desire to run away. We wish to run away to another world or fly to the heavens of the thirty-three devas, although we may not know what the Palace or the heavens look like. We do not know if it is cold or hot there or if there is no oxygen to breathe, or if there is no Vietnamese food like *Phở*, no Starbucks coffee, no carrots, no potatoes. You may not be able to see the beautiful sunrise on the top of the mountain, where one can see the sunset on the field full of scented flowers and green grass. Yet many of us are fleeing into the illusion of a world we do not know and leaving the reality of this real and beautiful world in which we are living.

The Buddha established an ideal environment immediately after he became enlightened. Many scriptures note that the formation of a flourishing community will bring happiness to many people.

"What have you heard, my friend: do people have frequent gatherings, and are their meetings well attended?

I have heard, Buddha, that this is so.

So long, my friend, as this is the case, the growth of the people is to be expected, not their decline.

What have you heard, my friend: do people assemble and disperse peacefully and attend to their affairs in concord?

I have heard, Buddha, that this is so.

So long, my friend, as this is the case, the growth of the people is to be expected, not their decline.

LIVING IN THE GOOD ENVIRONMENT

What have you heard, my friend: do people neither enact new decrees nor abolish existing ones, but proceed in accordance with their ancient constitutions?

I have heard, Buddha, that they do.

So long, my friend, as this is the case, the growth of the people is to be expected, not their decline.

What have you heard, Ananda: do people show respect, honor, esteem, and veneration towards their elders and think it worthwhile to listen to them?

I have heard, Buddha, that they do.

So long, my friend, as this is the case, the growth of people is to be expected, not their decline.

What have you heard, my friend: do people refrain from abducting women and maidens of good families and from detaining them?

I have heard, Buddha, that they refrain from doing so.

So long, Buddha, as this is the case, the growth of the people is to be expected, not their decline.

What have you heard, my friend: do people show respect, honor, esteem, and veneration towards their shrines, both those within the city and those outside it, and do not deprive them of the due offerings as given and made to them formerly?

I have heard, Buddha, that they do venerate their shrines, and that they do not deprive them of their offerings.

So long, my friend, as this is the case, the growth of the people is to be expected, not their decline.

What have you heard, my friend: do people duly protect and guard the arahats, so that those who have not come to the realm yet might do so, and those who have already come might live there in peace?

I have heard, Buddha, that they do.

So long, my friend, as this is the case, the growth of the people is to be expected, not their decline."[23]

It is easy to recognize an ideal place where the residents are united with respect for the law, respect for the intellectuals, and have great gratitude to their parents. Wherever the members are doing so, there is a sign of serenity, because the joy of happiness or despair of suffering affects the people in the environment. This is an ideal which today's society must apply.

In the sense of building a healthy community, the Buddha's sangha is the earliest community in the history of humanity that together studied and practiced religion. Through many experiences of self, the Buddha has built a community of living together in harmony for the common good of all people through the six acts of accord and respect.

The six acts of accord and respect are the steps towards a quality life for a person who has compassion, tolerance, harmony, material and spiritual protection in all aspects of life. Harmony has beautiful goals, benefits for themselves and for others; it is not passive, weak, competitive, or taking advantage of others.

51
LIVING IN THE GOOD ENVIRONMENT

The ideal environment, starts with the individual living in community, and extends to the family, spouses and children, brothers and sisters living in harmony, leading the family to be close and tight. In contrast, if the family does not reconcile, not only will they experience the loss of happiness, but the children will be affected by the anguish of the environment. In a neighborhood, if residents are not in accord with each other, then arguments and lawsuits, are born and the residents scramble to destroy each other. If organizations are not in harmony then it is hard to be successful and the possibility of disbandment can happen at any time, because there is no integration and mutual understanding. Therefore, apply the spirit of the six methods of accord and respect into daily life, as this will help you know how to love each other, to respect each other with compassion towards humanity.

The first accordance is performing the same practices as others, which means spirit is living in the same house, in a community, in an organization, always aware of the responsibilities, loving-and helping each other as much as possible. Do not use power to bully or harm others, but to love and support each other. Parents, brothers, sisters, children must respect each other to create a happy atmosphere.

The second accordance is the speech concord or kind speech, which means lovely, gracious speaking. Arguments will cause failure. Everyone has the right to express their opinions and has the right to contribute constructive ideas so that they can be better, but with a spirit of harmony, mutual learning, listening with compassion, and sharing with all the panels of love, gentleness and joy.

The third accordance is thinking concord or kindheartedness, or mental unity in faith, which means always being pleasant toward each other, sympathetic to each other, being happy when seeing other people's success, and helping with all your heart when you see others in difficult situations. Practice loving kindness, compassion, inner joy, perfect equanimity to help others increase energy, ignore others' mistakes, and be able to forgive easily.

The fourth accordance is precept concord, or observing the same precepts as others, or moral unity in observing the commandments, which means always observing precepts together. Those who live together in an environment and community must respect and practice the ethical principles taught and comply with the general rule.

The fifth accordance is idea concord, or sharing the same view as others, or doctrinal unity in views and explanations, which means always discussing and absorbing the Dharma together, sharing knowledge with each other, concentrating on establishing views, all thoughts being based on the common interest of the collective community. Share good knowledge to benefit others and bring common joy.

The sixth accordance is beneficial concord or economic unity in the community of goods, deeds, studies, or charity. Equality and harmony can be based on the position of each individual. However, all people should be equal, with the right to inherit material and spiritual freedom.

The six virtues of harmony are a moral norm for building a very peaceful and secure society. It is a jewel in itself, making an important contribution to a good society. According to sociologists, the largest proportion of successful children have been raised in a good environment. Attempting to cultivate a strong place of peace not only helps us to be happy but also brings a great future for the next generation. Look back and ask yourself how your surroundings are! "If you have a wise companion, you will overcome all dangers, live in happy mindfulness. If you do not have a wise companion, then you're just like a King that left the country, lonely like a forest elephant. It is better to live alone than associate with the bad influence of a friend."[24] Pay attention to this issue, because it affects your life dearly.

> *"Live in the good environment*
> *Take care of the heart garden*
> *Nourish the source of peace*
> *Boddhicitta will have a wonderful flower bloom."*

7

BEING CREATING GOOD SEEDS

"If you can listen to the teachings of love, compassion and Bodhicitta, these are the main ways to make your life truly peaceful. Even if you cannot do one hundred percent you can at least understand the value, and the good will always grow bigger and happier."

Humans cannot be separate from society to live alone in a solitary life, and even the herbaceous animals are like that. They have an interconnectedness to create life, as evident in the existence of humans and all other beings on this planet. Thus, wherever we go, under any circumstances, human beings always have a desire to survive, to escape suffering, and to seek happiness in life. Therefore, the existence of good ideas is essential in life, and spreading good will guide your life in a wonderful direction.

55
BEING CREATING GOOD SEEDS

A person whose mind is always thinking good thoughts will experience happiness in the present moment. There is one thing that everyone knows, which is that when we have the idea of creating great blessings and good deeds, these positive activities accumulate in the mind, these experiences will help us advance in life.

When you have strong motivation to do good thing for others, your mind is filled with joy and your life is full of meaning. When you always want to do things to benefit others, you will find that happiness is here and now. It is very practical that all the happiness you get, whether small or great, depends on the operation of the mind. In the depths of the mind, the more you care about others, the more happiness you feel. It is a natural law, because you have awakened the altruistic mind, and that altruism makes you happy.

The tendency to ignore the interests and benefits of others, thinking only of your own self-interests, will lead you to become lonely and less happy. If you maintain the kindness to help others, you will find peace in the present moment and it will benefit you in the future. A selfish attitude and tendency to leave others will result in misfortune for you. As such, for the same person, there is a clear difference between the level of consciousness and selfishness will destroy yourself and those around you. A person with a heart that cares about life and benefits others will bring happiness to himself and those around him. Thus, good deeds mean an arising of goodness of mind, and will be the source of good qualities in the present and in the future. The selfish and ignorant attitude is the cause of all suffering and leads to divergence from the path of peace and happiness.

The state of goodness is always in you, but your compassion must be raised. In other words, you must spread out the seeds of goodness, then the fruit of happiness will be present. Some enlightened masters, disciples of the Buddha, blamed themselves for failing to initiate and cultivate the seed of great compassion. Master Sariputta, one of the great disciples of the Buddha, had attained liberation, but Sariputta blamed himself: "In the course of practice in previous lives, I have allowed the deception of bad thoughts, so our future life will not teach the ultimate dharma in the three realms."[25] Sariputta blamed himself for not creating the good seeds, as he had the noble will to achieve the transcendent quality of the Tathāgata, in order to have ability to teach as the enlightened one. However, many documents in Buddhist literature say the Buddha taught the path of accomplishment simply: If you remain mindful, 'confess or have recitation to Buddha's name' in the places where the Buddha's teachings are, all these people, even once, have attained sublime wisdom.[26] Sometimes, being simple and brief can make it difficult for the recipient to perceive, therefore the Buddha proclaimed the following ethics: All elements are often quiet, naturally our true selves are calm, the Buddhists after the full realization, they will become the future Buddha.[27] This teaching marks a great event in the Buddha's theory. The cause and effect doctrine is recognized as the fair balance of human society and also the human standards of morality.

In Pali language, the phrase *Pubbe ca kata-puññatā*, is creating good causes. It means always look toward the direction of good, cultivate a lot of blessings to create happiness and dharma joy. All people from birth until cognitive maturity, desire to have a meaningful and beautiful life. Today, you can listen to the teachings of love, compassion, and Bodhi mind, how to make your life truly peaceful! Even if you cannot practice one hundred percent whole, but at least you understand the value of creating good causes, you always nurture the good will and it will grow bigger every day.

Mindfulness is the material that nourishes good seeds, because in every gesture your actions represent your personality. Therefore, take care of your thoughts as they become your words and deeds; Take care of your actions as they may become your habit; Take care of your habits as they will form your character; Take care of your character as it will shape your destiny; And your destiny will be your life." The mind must be well-cared for, gradually changing negative minds full of thoughts like anger, jealousy, selfishness, and envy, to minds of compassion. And we must be brave, recognize other people's suffering, and care more about the interests of others than ourselves.

Looking at the masters that have led the holy life, they have contributed much work to the benefit of life and brought more peace to society, which is the way to sow good seeds. The example is a motivating force for promoting the cultivation of noble, pure seeds in which the aspiration of a great compassionate mind develops. Bodhicitta is nourished every day, so you will have more peace and more happiness in life.

Belief in the Buddha's teachings has launched, because the Dharma has the power to transform suffering, bring peace, and liberate delusion. Believing in the power of love can transform difficulties and conquer the hearts of others.

The Buddha taught how to practice in a way that supports happiness and creates blessings. "Dear children, there are methods for the growth of goodwill, great blessings, great retribution, great honor, great merit.

Dear friends, good men or faithful women who have faith in offering the land, housing, accommodation, rooms, beds, tools, mattresses, weaving, woolen blankets, for the monks. It is a great blessing, great retribution, great honor, great merit.

Again, good men and faithful women who have the devotion to the monasteries of the disciples of the Buddha who are residing, with joy, happiness, excitement, and through study, apply these to daily life. Their blessings cannot be calculated, no matter how long the blessing, we can only say there is no limit, no way to quantify, no calculation of the number of blessings."

It is easy to see why the Buddha taught how to create a good cause by providing spiritual offerings to homeless or those poor who need help, because it is a very concrete way of practicing. These are yours and so easy to do. When your mind is thinking of others, it raises the will to share, and the seed of compassion in you is nourished and happiness is present. The saints are lauded and praised, praised not because they have physical strength, but because they have a loving heart, giving shelter to others. Light the torch of wisdom with mindful awareness every day to burn the torch in your heart to bring peace to you and to many others.

> *"Created good effect*
> *Growth of great of mind compassion*
> *Light up the torch of wisdom*
> *Make peace of life."*

8

GUIDING OUR MIND TOWARD THE RIGHTEOUS PATH

"The safest protection over anyone is myself. Self-illuminate the mind by practicing mindfulness every day. Mindfulness is the energy that is capable of recognizing anything that is happening now and here."

Old religions, as well as today, have many differences in teaching methods and ways of approaching people, but the basis of these religions is that they pointed to the basic truth of the practitioner of righteousness; that it is healthy to create joy and happiness in life. If the mind is not trained, or is careless, then the mind becomes wild, old, and does not continue to grow.

With regard to mind, Christianity states that the normal psychological state of every human being is mostly of *original sin*.[28] On semantics, *Sin* means doing moral wrong, as the archer does not hit the target, so the arrow goes in the wrong direction. So *sin* can be understood as a mistake, or not the right purpose of a human life. This means that the person has lived in confusion, living in blindness, lacking intelligence, is not clever, and has a mind obscured by darkness. This causes personal suffering and suffering for many others. Thus, the word "Sin" implies alienation, ignorant cover up, and is always present in the human condition.

No one can deny that the century we are living in witnesses the great achievement of science and technology. Humans have created wonderful music, architecture, art, literature, and painting masterpieces that are beyond imagination. In the last few decades, modern science and technology have devised intelligent tools that have radically changed the way we live our lives. These tools include: Skype – a free online tool that allows users to talk using video calls; Facebook – a friendly social network for communication and connection; YouTube - the world's largest video library; Nintendo Wii – a home gaming console that incorporates real movements into the digital experience; Smartphones – touchscreen devices with endless applications simulating a digital world at your fingertips; Netflix – an online media platform that enables users to watch movies and television ad free and on demand; Amazon Kindle – a handheld tablet that brings the library to you, wherever you go; Spotify –-an online music streaming service, giving gives users an access to a wealth of music; 4G – the provision of data for a fast Internet connection speed. In the next few years, Tesla and many other companies will produce automatic automobiles without human drivers. Already meetings and conferences are connected online via the Internet. Hundreds of years ago, these things were unimaginable and would have been considered a miracle. The human mind is amazing. However, it is also the intelligence of modern tools that can pollute humanity, through insanity and loss of control of the mind. Technological engineering has interfered deeply with human life, exaggerating the effects of destructive power on the environment and on humanity itself. Indeed, the consequences are alarming.

The lush green forests that feed clean air to the planet are all being destroyed, the animals are helpless and hunted; this and many more poses as a danger to the human race. The planet is warming up and the weather has become erratic. This is the result of humans' selfishness and greed. Consequently, this has led to a lack of awareness of the intimate relationship between man and nature, and his pursuit of unrighteous actions, if uncontrolled, will lead to the disappearance of the human race in the near future.

Anxiety, fear, the desire for power, and selfish longings are the psychological motives behind people doing bad things. This unwholesome mind not only causes personal conflicts, but causes war and violence among nations, tribes, ideologies, and even within religions. Unrighteous minds create distortion in how you think about other people, and even yourself. It is this motivation that misleads you to do foolish and insane actions. The attempt to get rid of the fear and anxiety results in additional wrongdoings, taking you further away from the righteous path. If there is a purpose, then it only strengthens selfishness and the accumulation of wealth for yourself. But the essence of wanting to accumulate is just like a deep valley with no bottom, as you will never fill it up and be satisfied.

It is important that you realize the fear, the anxiety, the craving for power, and the desire that lives in you. In other words, it is necessary to recognize the unwholesome mind. Many methods have been put out by psychologists and sociologists to counter the anger and fear of humans by letting these patients into a room where they can get rid of the affliction of fear by smashing the things that you normally do not dare to do because of the fear of affecting others or fear of physical damage. These methods can reduce the anger for a short time, but cannot eradicate it deep within the mind. The Buddha taught that you must learn to train the mind to keep the mind in the righteous way (*atta sammā panidhi ca*). *Atta* is *mine, self*, also called *ego*. Our mind is often referred to as a waterfall, always flowing, or just like monkeys jumping from one branch to other, never standing still. The mind does not stop thinking throughout the day, and even at night the mind is very active. Sometimes it arises with righteous thoughts, but sometimes the unrighteous mind cannot be controlled, and the moment the disturbing mind arises it makes us lose direction and causes suffering for ourselves and others.

The Buddha said: "Those who engage in good conduct of body, speech, and mind protect themselves. Even though no company of elephant troops protects them, nor a company of cavalry, nor a company of charioteers, nor a company of infantry, still they protect themselves. For what reason? Because that protection is internal, not external; therefore, they protect themselves." [29]

The safest protection is self-protection; Self-illuminate the mind by practicing mindful awareness every day. Mindfulness is the energy that is capable of recognizing anything that is happening now and here. In the Chinese character (念) for the word *mindfulness*, the top portion of character (念) is (今) which means the present moment; the bottom portion of the character (念) is (心), which means your heart. Mindfulness is what you are thinking and remembering to be in the present moment. Mindfulness means righteousness, goodness in the heart; it helps you to hold thoughts, emotions, feelings, and see your surroundings in every moment, but only identify them without judging if they are right or wrong.

Intentional action in Pali is *manasikara* and is one of the fifty-one metal formations, which means initiating the mind to pay attention to the object. Being previously unfocused and shifting to pay attention is called intentional action. It is one of the five universal mental formations (touch, attention, feeling, perception, and volition). It starts with a thought. When you read a book or watch a movie, the image on the page or in that movie can form the intentional action. If there is reflection and practice then it becomes good intentions, good actions.

Also, that image can make you have deliberate wrong and evil ideas. When one is interested in an event or object, if that object is in line with the spirit of respect for life, the protection of the environment, bringing joy to many people, this is literally called systematic attention, which means doing-in-the-mind. It requires constant awareness of the things that one meets with in everyday life (*yoniso manaskara*). The opposite is not systematic attention (*ayoniso manaskara*). Yoniso is a Pali term which means by-way-of-womb instead of only on the surface. Therefore, systematic attention means a radical or reasoned attention. Yoni in the Chinese language is the womb, or the palace of the child. Yoni means root. When returning to the right source, not distracted, it is called Yoniso.

Life has many temptations to cause you to forget mindfulness, like watching an action movie, in which the content of the movie tends to create erroneous thinking, which is not systematic attention. Therefore, in daily life you need to practice mindfulness to illuminate your mind as a logical mind. Mindfulness is the birth of the mind towards the right path. Awareness is a kind of energy to light up the mind, bringing us back to ourselves. Then, your actions are consistent with the path, leading you to the path of happiness, and freeing yourself from suffering, which is the greatest happiness in life.

> *"The mind is in the right direction*
> *All our spoken words and actions*
> *Are nurtured and protected*
> *Happiness is here and now."*

9

PROFOUND KNOWLEDGE

"The purpose of learning and practicing Buddhism is to help one live in the present, or consciously focus on the present moment. It is in the here and now that life is occurring. The powerful magic thus belongs to the present. Imagine if one loses touch with the present, we would be deprived of the power to live, the ability to enjoy life. Our life would be wasted!"

The founder of Buddhism, Siddhartha, was a prince of the royal Sakya clan. The Buddha grew up in a kingdom and received an extraordinary education. The broad knowledge learned from this time brought him great success later in life when he taught his Dharma to the people of different cultures, ethnicities, and religions in India. Researchers have determined that the Buddha spoke different languages to different ethnicities. His preaching journey covered all over the Ganges River area. The Buddha's words were documented in scriptures.

They demonstrated his insights into science, politics, psychology, sociology, education, and other subjects. Up to this day, scientists are astonished by his great wisdom and hence inspired to learn more about Buddhism.

The Buddha's teaching came into existence to serve people and is a necessity to people's lives. He taught us that our suffering stems from mistakes made in our own course of thinking and action. At the same time, he showed us the way to self-liberation and happiness, encouraging our non-stop learning. Unfortunately, only a few people truly grasp his Dharma. The majority either ignore or misconstrue his teachings. For centuries, numerous Buddhist monks have added their own ideas in their sermons, steering away or completely separating from the Buddha's teaching. The enlightened man aimed his Dharma for decongestion of human minds, trying to cure the insanity that spins many around the vicious cycles of suffering.

It would be a grave mistake to think Buddhism is meant only for monastics who live an isolated life in the woods or on top of a mountain, and to assume that all they have to do is meditate and chant. It would also be wrong to think of Buddhism merely as a stack of sutras, a static theory that does not adapt to the complexity of life. Not at all! Buddhism was founded to work with human life. Therefore, Buddhism is just as dynamic as our life in the ever-changing world. For that reason, it would be a misconception to view Buddhism as an artifact or antique exhibited in a museum that might reveal some details of an ancient life and has nothing to do with our own.

In the history of Buddhism, there were cases where the religion was undermined by undereducated monks who mis-rendered the Buddha's words to the public. Consequently, few people attended Buddhist temples regardless of how monumental and luxuriously these temples were built. ~~to become.~~ Only a few superstitious elders came to pray for blessing or to seek fortune-telling. But the majority of the young generation and the intellects were absent. It was not the people's intention to abandon their traditional religion. It was simply because the sermons did not address their needs and failed to provide guidelines on how to deal with daily problems. The preaching and the chanted words were too hard to understand.

For both individuals and communities, it is a necessity to learn matters that help life. This is especially true in modern society. The discussion of the Dharma in this area must be related to modern lifestyles. Let us view the ancient Buddhism from the angle of our contemporaries and teach the religion with that regard. Practicing Buddhism is about applying its essential philosophy to our daily life. It is not about following the religion exactly to tradition, as it was followed in the ancient time. Let us utilize our best analysis and tools to bring Buddhism to life in the 21st century.

First of all, keep in mind that learning Buddhism is not the same as touring a historical museum, after which one could boast with friends for having seen the world's most beautiful antiques. On the contrary, learning Buddhism requires understanding the important role it plays in humanity. One should envision the livelihood Buddhism would bring to individuals as well as society. With that mentality, we can grasp the Buddha's magic words even though they are just echoes from twenty-six centuries ago, and the Dharma can be practically helpful to all lives. With that thought process, we will be aware of our mission as Buddhists in society. From there we can successfully perpetuate the religion.

Bahusacca in Pali language means "great learning or profound knowledge," which is the subject of discussion in this chapter. *Bahusacca* is an important quality for a layperson to have because he must be able to understand the true meaning of Buddha's word in order to learn his methodologies and to practice them properly. *Bahusacca* is even more important for monks because they need it for preaching. Indeed, they have to undergo a long professional training in order to master all aspects of the religion. Psychology, sociology, philosophy and like areas of knowledge are required of trainees for their graduation to become monks.

Learning Buddhist wisdom either as a layperson or as a monk, we should often ask ourselves: What have we learned from the Buddha's teaching? Which practice have we adopted? Does the Dharma provide any practical solutions? Does it help us reduce suffering and increase happiness?

There are countless people who recite sutras daily and have learned Buddhism for years. Some even know most words in a Buddhist dictionary, being able to elaborate the meanings of most terminology. However, many of them fail the most import part: practice. The knowledge acquired never gets to be applied. Therefore, there is no wisdom obtained. Instead of enjoying the vigorous life force brought by Buddhism, they choose to hold on to the antique-like part of the religion: the beautiful old-aged literature. Such a mistake does not get practitioners anywhere. The mispractice is almost like entertaining oneself by touring a historic museum. It is so in the sense that both activities stem from the love for antiques or old-aged literature. Worst of all, when learning Buddhism without practice, one inadvertently sends a negative message to the world, that the Dharma is a joke, incapable of improving life. Whereas the museum touring activity is harmless, mispractice of Buddhism could be a harmful blasphemy.

Cases of mispractice are not unique. We observe characters that preach Buddhism a lot, and yet live their lives as if they have never seen the light of the Dharma joy. That sad situation is like a spoon sitting inside a pot of delicious soup. The spoon never gets to taste the rich flavor of the soup despite the fact that it is submerged in the broth. To avoid the mispractice set forth, one needs to learn Buddhism with the determination of a truth seeker, with the heart of an artist who admires beauty, with the anxiety of a patient in need of a doctor, or with the thirst of a lost person in a desert. Only with one of those drives can one find the wonder of the Buddha's words.

To illustrate the mispractice of Buddhism, the story of Ananda was told. Ananda was among the great students of the Buddha. With a supreme mental capacity, he was able to record his teacher's words by memory, missing none. According to written history, the process of his learning from the Buddha was like how water is poured into one glass from another without spilling. Ananda was highly respected by peers for his special learning ability. However, in failing to apply the broad knowledge, he did not obtain self-liberation. He did not reach the spiritual level where he could set himself free from sufferings via detachment from the ego and materialistic objects in life. Left behind because of the mispractice, he was not admitted to the first sutra convention. It took him quite some time to clear up the obstacles in his spiritual path. Finally, with great effort of practice, he was admitted to the convention.

Addressing the mispractice, the Buddha often clarified for his students that pointing his finger to the moon must not be confused for the moon. The finger was used to show the direction to the moon, but itself was not the target. The Dharma is aimed at helping us recognize our selfness, to connect deeply with our consciousness, and to be in touch with the present. These targets are also shared among multiple religions under different names. They are called the Buddha nature in Buddhism, the nature of God in Christianity, or Atman in Hinduism. Like many other religions, Buddhism is intended to show people the way to happiness.

Ironically, many misconstrue the Buddha's intention, seeing his finger as the moon instead of following the direction to which it was pointing. The pointing finger symbolizes the Dharma, the Buddha's instruction which became the literature part of Buddhism. Unfortunately, many of us often get caught up in this literature part, failing to apply the teaching therein. Emphasizing sutra study and setting aside practice, one could end up being lost in the mess of arguments, concepts, and language. This issue often causes mental congestion, blinding us to the Buddha nature. However, if we deeply understand the Buddha's intention and apply his teaching accordingly, we will gather a power that nourishes life. Practicing the Dharma, we will be uplifted beyond the limitations of our body and mind.

The esoteric parts of Buddhist literature could be difficult to understand. As sophisticated as some texts or teachings might appear, they could end up bringing more confusion than help to some individuals. Not only could the complicated teachings be ineffective in easing our misery, they could also adversely become obstacles against our finding happiness. This risk could be associated with

Bahusacca or profound knowledge. The problem occurs when one cannot clearly distinguish means from purpose. Indeed, it is critically important for us to be alert to the fact that the Dharma itself is only a tool, whereas achieving the Buddha nature via consciously practicing the teaching is the ultimate goal.

The purpose of learning and practicing Buddhism is to help one live in the moment, or consciously focus on the present. It is in the here and now that life is occurring. The powerful magic thus belongs to the present. Imagine if one loses touch with the present; he would be deprived of the power to live, the ability to enjoy life. His life would be wasted. In understanding such purpose of learning and meaningfulness of practice, we shall avoid mispractice. Then it will be safe to indulge ourselves in learning all the Buddhist literature we wish. It is so because at any breath you take, there will no longer be the confusion about the means for the purpose, about the finger for the moon.

Technically the claim above is valid. We can learn and practice Buddhism successfully. However, there are only a few of us who successfully stay conscious during our practice. As intelligent as humans are, our psychology still reveals a lack of spiritual consciousness. This issue is characterized by discontents, or the dissatisfactory feelings towards what we have in the moment. As a result, people constantly seek to play, to do something fun, or to learn something for the sake of excitement. On the other hand, people also constantly run away from loneliness, hopelessness, or even themselves. These behaviors are simply the phenomena of mental imbalance and lack of self-awareness. They become habits, carrying on from the past to the present.

Habits are hard to break. We tend to carry the same baggage to our practice. The lacking consciousness issue becomes manifest when we are determined that learning extra Buddhist knowledge is mandatory. It is a must to memorize the whole Buddhist dictionary, a must to study the Zen traditional, or a must to study the Emptiness, etc. Although this determination is a great tool for success, it can be manipulated by the ego at the deep level of consciousness. Dealing with this issue, the Buddha taught that nibbana can only be achieved in the absence of this self-centering characteristic. Feeding the ego only steers us away from peace and happiness.

The natural state of mind is emptiness. In this state, the mind is characterized by peace, brilliance and spatial infinity. That is the mental state that we wish to strive for. The empty mind opens us to life events, allowing us to perceive them with accuracy and without bias. Achieving this high consciousness, one lives in the moment. On the contrary, the preoccupied mind strips away our direct contact with life. It does so by tying us to certain objects that the mind reflects in itself, separating us from reality. Losing direct contact with life, one loses the factors necessary for survival.

However, losing the empty mind is a common problem. Although Buddhist practitioners are supposed to work on clearing their mental clouds, the outcome sometimes is the opposite. They might end up clinging more to their ego, losing peace and wisdom along the way. The following story is an example of the irony. There once was an old lady, a devout Buddhist who participated in weekly temple charity work, and she never missed reciting Buddhist sutras any day. She also contributed a large portion of her income to the building project of a famous temple. Assuming a higher status for the work she had done, she became unpleasant. Pride stripped away her respect for other people. Then one day a neighbor came to visit. Standing from outside, he heard the sound of her ritual. Yet he still rang the doorbell, hoping to learn what her reaction would be. After the first series of three rings, she did not respond. The sounds of the wooden bell and the singing bowl from her shrine still went on steadily. As two minutes went by, he tried again. This time, the sounds of the wooden bell and singing bowl started to go haywire. He tried a third time. Finally, she could not compose herself any longer. Dropping her ritual, she ran out to fight with the visitor. She hysterically screamed at him: "Hey you, old man, are you deaf? You are vexing me, disturbing my ritual." Bombarded by her anger, he calmly stood still until she calmed down. Then he tenderly spoke to her: "If my ringing the bell for three times drives you so mad, how angry do you think the Buddha would be at you for calling his name at the altar daily?"

Learning and practicing Buddhism improperly, we might inadvertently end up being more attached to our ego. In turn, the attachment to the ego inflicts stagnation upon our spiritual path. Paradoxically, this issue appears to relate to high social status and success. The issue goes hand in hand with the aspects of fame and fortune. Were we part of the humble class without fame or power, our ego would have little chance to manifest itself. It would appear as if the ego does not exist. On the contrary, the ego of successful people tends to be evident. It is so because their ego is constantly at stake. Multiple factors can cause damage to their self-respect. The culprits lie in characteristics such as power, fame, money, pride, etc. These materialistic entities feed on the ego, and at the same time they are subjected to change and destruction. When the feeding of the ego no longer happens, it is damaged, resulting in people's mental and emotional distress. These types of suffering tend to be deeper and longer-lasting than physical ones. Therefore, when the damage to the ego occurs, people tend to fight vigorously to eliminate their opponents. Discovering the sadness of "fame and fortune" as well as the ego's relationship with them, we come to realize that the so-called happiness brought by the materialistic entities is delusional. Because of their artificial nature, fame and fortune are incapable of bringing true happiness.

We often recognize the attachment-to-the-ego issue with high-status people such as professors at a prestigious university, famous doctors, or celebrities. Among Buddhists, a highly ranked person such as an abbot who is in charge of an abbey can also be found sensitive to criticism. A similar story was told about a pastor of a famous parish in a big city. Every Friday evening, he preached a sermon after prayers. The pastor misspoke of God's magic at the sermon. He said, "Jesus, when granting His blessing to the people, had 1000 loaves of bread to give one man." Yet God still had 999 left on hand. The details conflicts with the bible. Supposedly, Christ had only one loaf of bread, and yet he was able to give 1000 people one loaf each. After all, according to the bible, He still had one loaf left. Normally churchgoers would not dare to correct any mistake made by the respected pastor. However, that Friday, a dull farmer was present, and things were different. Spotting the mistake, the man instantly stood up and questioned the pastor. Embarrassed, the priest responded promptly just to brush off tension. Deep down inside, he was angry for being corrected.

The following Friday, the pastor preached the same story. This time being well prepared, he told the story correctly. At the end, the pastor suddenly turned to the farmer and asked him with a sarcastic tone: "My friend, you think you could do the same magic Christ did?" The farmer responded by making fun of the priest, mentioning the misspoken detail of the 999 loafs of bread left over on Christ's hands. He said to the priest: "Indeed, I can. And anybody in this room can too. One loaf of bread today plus 999 left over from the last time you said, that will total 1000."

Besides entertaining readers with the twist at the end, the story also brings a moral. The lesson is, had the pastor not taken the farmer's words personally, he would have skipped the hassle of fighting and avoided the embarrassment. Apologizing for a mistake despite its triviality would have been a smart choice. Usually, clinging to the ego blinds people to the truth. Strong attachment to this self-respect tends to bring conflicts, hatred, and even wars. The Buddha probably was among the first to recognize this issue in humans. He taught that in the absence of the ego, nibbana is obtained. Jesus also preached the same. That is, one should abandon one's own ego. Due to the absence of self-respect an awakened person is highly conscious. She or he is well aware of life events via senses and thought processes. With high awareness, the person comes to realize that fame and status are just labels which are artificial or not real. Recognizing the unreal, one detaches oneself from illusions. This leaves the person in direct contact with life.

Does Bahusacca, or profound knowledge, help eliminate illusions so that one can find the truth? It is certainly helpful, yet the outcome still depends. Let us take precaution by first doing a risk assessment. The risk is, once the ego is set free to feed on profound knowledge, it grows to become an obstacle against our spiritual growth. Like a cloud over a mountain, it blinds us to the truth.

Allowing the ego to combine with profound knowledge, we might end up with religious fanaticism. Cases of religious narcissism are quite common. We often know of Buddhist practitioners who claim to be students of an honorific Lama, a well-known Dharma teacher, or a famous Zen master. Claiming to have attended the teaching of one of these Buddhist celebrities, the practitioners would boast that their master is the best. Normally, pride taken for one's own knowledge, academic degree, or achievement is justifiable by her or his hard work. To some extent, that sort of pride is acceptable. On the contrary, taking pride for the achievement by someone else, the credit of one's teacher in this case, is among the most pitiful examples of attachment to the ego. In Buddhism, profound knowledge without application or practice is not far from complete ignorance of the Dharma. In order to avoid such a mispractice, we must be well aware of who we are. We must never attach ourselves tightly to any doctrine, school of thought, temple, or master. The attachment eventually becomes an obstacle against our spiritual growth.

Setting aside the risk assessed above, the bigger picture is that profound knowledge tends to benefit individuals, family and society. Psychologists determine that highly educated people tend to make good decisions and solve problems successfully. Also, people with high intellect tend to take care of themselves well and often lend hands to others. Interestingly, researchers observe the positive relation between education and lifespan. Indeed, college-educated individuals tend to live up to 80 years, whereas their high-school-level counterparts average a lifespan that is three years shorter. Neurologists have discovered a strong link between education and the social, physical, and psychological well-being of a person. They find that great learning helps one avoid multiple illness. For example, people who read daily greatly reduce their risk of hearing loss, Alzheimer's disease, or other types of dementia.

From the spiritual point of view, profound knowledge has the potential to bring success and happiness. People who attend Buddhist training classes tend to be highly driven. They are ready to practice what they learn and wish to learn even more. With open consciousness, they feel an urge to help themselves and others. If a person happened to get lost in the past, she would be re-directed to find herself. Under the light of the Dharma, people are driven to work their lives towards a brighter future and to help others to do the same. Profound knowledge, when applied, becomes great wisdom. Wisdom in turn is capable of life redemption. *Bahusacca*, therefore, is what we should strive for on our spiritual path. People often learn the Dharma in training classes. If that is the case, it is advisable that students be in touch with the masters, mingle with other students in class, and be open to the methodology offered by the Dharma. Success is waiting for them down the line.

The enthusiasm to learn and the longing for the truth drives students towards success. The inspiration sparked by a Buddhist master plays a very important role in encouragement for the students. The master's broad knowledge in language, tradition, and culture are necessary for bringing out the zeal in learners. Language skills are particularly important. They are essential for the master to have in order to effectively share his knowledge and experience to all students.

Indeed, *profound knowledge* depends greatly on language. Humans use language to communicate and to learn. The sound of language has been used to speak the magic truth, which transforms consciousness. By means of language, the Buddha's teaching was first taught more than 2,500 years ago. Generations thereafter, his teaching have been learned and taught also via language. Because of the inevitability of language, the ability to communicate should be mastered as part of *profound knowledge* as well. Being strong at language skills, one can share her knowledge and experience of the Dharma to others, bringing more happiness to life.

There is knowledge which can increase the self's ego. We should always be aware of this and confirm what we know and what we have learned with the reality of the here and now. Because of the impermanance in this world, our knowledge of the environment must be changed. If the knoweldge is not up-to-date, one may be trapped into false perception, which leads to prejudice and misconception. The mistakes from misconception leads to suffering for the self and others. That is harmful knowledge.

PROFOUND KNOWLEDGE

Thanks to the existence of language, Buddhism has been passed a long way to our generation. One would wonder if there must be a reason for the Dharma to carry on for two and a half millennia. Indeed, the ancient treasure of knowledge has been useful to people of all times, providing practical solutions to their problems. When taught to people, the Dharma tends to help clear up their minds. Mental congestion, attachment to the ego, or any other obstacles should disappear under the light of the Buddhist teachings. Listening to a sermon or reading a sutra should lighten up the practitioners' spirit. They tend to feel happier. If that is the case, the practitioners are moving towards the right direction. Eventually, they will be empowered with wisdom so they can help others. In the end, the practitioners will find peace and live in the moment.

Although they can be nicely sparked from the Dharmic study set forth, peace and happiness demand daily effort to maintain. It takes learning along the way. In order to sustain a tranquil and joyous state of mind, we must nourish positive thoughts, just like farmers nourishing good seeds in their lands. Most importantly, keep in mind the basic guideline for bringing peace and happiness. That is, chaos brings the urge to establish peace, and suffering is the fertile soil in which to grow happiness.

With daily learning and practicing, eventually wisdom will develop, compassion will grow, and life will become richer. The thriving process occurs like that of a young tree. The tree roots itself deeply into the soil to get the nutrients it needs. Eventually it will bloom, produce fruits, and bring fresh air to the environment. Similarly, in the spiritual world, our great training effort is aimed at nourishing our spirit, bringing peace and happiness. Eventually, the positivity can be shared with friends and family.

> *"Profound knowledge to be grasped*
> *The great Dharma joy to be learned*
> *Whoever reveres and follows*
> *His spirits will be lifted."*

10
RIGHT PROFESSIONS

> *"Not only does Buddhism help practitioners improve their spiritual matters such as personality, behavior, morality, but it also duly addresses the subject of socioeconomics. A hungry man needs food rather than meditation. Therefore, the Dharma regards the professional aspect in parallel with virtue."*

Profound knowledge is greatly important for uplifting spirits. On the other hand, food, clothing, housing, medicine, and other material items are equally important for sustaining life. Simply put, peace and happiness depend on both spiritual and material aspects. Emphasizing the well-rounded development of humans, Buddhism addresses spiritual health, bodily fitness, and economy. It considers right professions not only important to supporting life, but also fundamental for social development. It views right professions as the leverage for spiritual development as well.

Not only does Buddhism help practitioners improve spiritual characteristics such as personality, behavior, and morality, but it also duly addresses the subject of socioeconomics. A hungry man needs food rather than meditation. Therefore, the Dharma regards the professional aspect in parallel with virtue. The Buddha said: "All living beings rely on food to survive." The teaching exemplifies the pragmatic aspect of Buddhism. *Sippam*, in Pali language, means a mechanical art, fine art, a piece of work, a job, skills, or proficiency.

Sippam is an attribute of humans. Ancient people used their hands to seek foods from nature to provide for themselves and their family. Since civilization began, work has been performed more in terms of producing goods and earning profits. To accomplish those missions, we are gifted with a strong urge to gain goods or profits. However, the desire for material things at times misleads us to a wrong career path, driving us to do the type of work that hurts ourselves or other living beings. One should consciously avoid such unethical professions in order to prevent suffering in the future.

Regarding right professions, the Dharma joy specifically calls for our awareness and actions as follows: (1) Consciously protect the environment and the lives of people, animals, and plants. (2) Consciously protect people's love and marriage. (3) Avoid stealing, committing fraud, and treating others unfairly. Practice helping the poor via thought, speech and action. Although, they sound simplistic, those three suggestions are fundamental. They are crucial for peace and happiness for society.

RIGHT PROFESSIONS

Additionally, the Buddha taught the means of wealth: (1) One makes oneself happy and pleased and properly maintains oneself in happiness; (2) one makes one's parents happy and pleased and properly maintains them in happiness; (3) one makes one's wife and children, slaves, workers, and servants happy and pleased and properly maintains them in happiness; (4) one makes one's friends and companions happy and pleased and properly maintains them in happiness; (5) one establishes for ascetics and brahmins an uplifting offering of alms that is heavenly, resulting in happiness, and conducive to heaven. These are the five benefits of wealth.[30]

With an "honest work for honest pay" mentality and the aim to benefit ourselves and others, right professions will follow. Binding the pay and work obligation together, Zen master Baizhang said: "A day off work is like a day going hungry". Besides the value of honest work for honest pay expressed by master Bach Truong, most importantly keep in mind that the high values associated with right professions stem from compassion. Because compassion has the power–to eliminate suffering, to bring happiness, and even to fix mistakes, right professions have those powers as well.

> *"With the right profession*
> *Wherever one goes*
> *He gets the respect*
> *Such a fantastic man!"*

11

PRACTICING ETHICS

"Applying disciplines or precepts to the daily life helps one be aware of things happening around him, including his feelings and mental formations. This course of action helps prevent him from harming himself, others, the environment, and society. In addition, it protects one from being in the dark, being lost and guarantees a bright future with authentic peace and happiness"

In order to maintain an existence of an organization, there must be regulations and rules in place. Cabinet members of a government or a group of people must be established with the same concept. People come together for mutual benefit and to develop profit or materials, and they must have a set of rules. Buddha's Sangha was also built on rules that help individuals from different backgrounds live together with respect and in harmony.

Let's define the word *precept* in Buddhism. It comes from the word *sila* in Pali. *Sila* means nature, character, habit, or behavior. It also means moral practice, good character, Buddhist ethics, and code of morality.

Sila means the reality with its natural rules of operations, such as one's natural reaction to things in life. *Sila* has the capability to remind one when he exceeds the limits or rules and to prevent him from damaging others. For example, if one has eaten too much, he will be obese or sick. Similarly, if one steals goods from others, he will be punished by the law. In order to achieve a moral standard, and cause no harm to self and others, one must practice mindfulness to avoid breaking the natural rules of life. He must notably consider right from wrong to avoid troubles. Every moment he must contemplate what needs to be done. The meaning of *sila* is to help one live in happiness, to enable a group of people maintain order and morality. One lives his life by following precepts, staying peaceful, and avoiding conflict and suffering. He is said to be practicing *sila*.

Sila is as known as the first of Threefold Training in Buddhism: mindfulness, meditations, and wisdoms/insight. It is a principle morality or a way of life that fits within the natural laws. Chinese translators considered *sila* as a processes of purifying one's actions, speech, and mind. *Vinaya* are rules and regulations to guide people to return to their naturally peaceful lifestyle. Because people often cross the natural limits and violate laws of the land, *sila* or *vinaya* are set to reduce or adjust people's behaviors.

Buddha said: "After a Buddha has attained final nibbana, the bhikkhus, bhikkhunis, male lay followers, and female lay followers dwell with reverence and deference toward the Teacher. They dwell with reverence and deference toward the Dhamma. They dwell with reverence and deference toward the Sangha. They dwell with reverence and deference toward the training. They dwell with reverence and deference toward each other. This is the cause and reason why the good Dhamma continues long after a Tathagata has attained final nibbana."[31] The disciplines are to adjust the outer lives of Buddhists. Perhaps, this is why Buddha called his disciples, who strictly comply to rules, the solemn people. Disciplines are like flower rings one puts on a respected person. In another sutra, Buddha had said that "the fragrance of flowers drifts with the wind as sandalwood, jasmine, or lavender. The fragrance of the virtuous sweeps the wind; all pervasive is virtue of the good. Sandalwood or lavender, lotus or the great jasmine, of these many fragrances virtue's fragrance is supreme."[32] The brightness of an emperor who wears many valuable jewels has nothing to compare to that of a person who practices disciplines. Shine as they may, there are no kings, adorned with jewelry and pearls, that shine as does a man restrained, adorned with virtue's ornament. Virtue entirely does away with dread of self-blame and the like; The good of the virtuous gives gladness always by its fame.³³ Practicing disciplines maintains a person's self-control and makes joy in life.

Practicing ethics helps one to return to the natural life with less desires. This way of life gives people freedom from being attached. Therefore, *sila* is considered the source of happiness and peace. It is the starting point of enlightenment. Buddha had emphasized that controlling the activities of body, mouth, and mind prevents one from being evil; doing no wrong leads to no regret; no regret leads to joy; a joyful mind leads to blessedness; blessedness leads to mindfulness; mindfulness leads to wisdom; wisdom leads to freedom from attachment; detachment leads to the absence of greed; the absence of greed leads to liberation from selfishness; a liberated mind leads to liberated wisdom; wisdom leads to nibbana.³⁴

Commandments were set as shields to protect people on the road to contentment. Buddha created rules for his disciples and the followers to achieve this goal. He said: "I created commandments for the disciples because of the following benefits: bringing cheer and joy to people, preventing wrong doing, observing self actions. Commandments have power to control attachments to money, beauty, fame, eating and sleeping. They can protect people from resentments, mistakes, fears, and wrongdoing in the present and the future." ³⁵

Buddha also said: "Dear all, I teach the Dhamma that is good in the beginning, good in the middle, and good in the end, with the right meaning and phrasing; he reveals the perfectly complete and pure spiritual life. This is the Fortunate One's discipline. Thus, while the Fortunate One or the Fortunate One's discipline remains in the world, this is for the welfare of many people, for the happiness of many people, out of compassion for the world, for the good, welfare, and happiness of devas and humans.[36]

Sila has the power of training the mind. It helps to gain mindfulness to moderate one's feeling. It is the key to freedom, gratification and contentment. Once we have control over the body, the mouth, and the mind, we will gain freedom and satisfaction wherever we go. For example, if one is addicted to alcohol, or drugs, he depends on these things and loses his freedom. If he does not have money to buy alcohol or drugs, he will do anything to get them. He is said to be controlled by drugs or alcohol. He loses the freedom of mind and does things that he does not want to do. He becomes involved in criminal activities and imprisonment is the result. On the other hand, if one practices *sila*, he realizes alcohol can cause sickness and mental disorder. Once he understands, he can happily say no to drugs and alcohol.

To practice the moral life is to protect one's own freedom. Once he reaches his limits, one realizes that he is stepping into freedom. Each discipline gives him a different aspect of freedom. Five disciplines give five freedoms; ten disciplines give ten freedoms; two hundred and fifty disciplines give two hundred and fifty freedoms.

PRACTICING ETHICS

Morality is not limited within a party, or a religion. It covers the whole universe and is the authentic practice of compassion and wisdom. Most traditional spiritual practitioners have their principles to guide them, to prevent people from doing wrong, and to keep them away from social temptations. The five Mindfulness trainings of Buddhism are considered the basic morality rules for all. The First Precept is to reduce pain, anger, and vengeance between individuals, within family, and society. The Second Precept is to practice respect for individuals and their property; i.e., no stealing from others. The Third Precept is to protect virtue in marriage, to maintain family and to raise children in the best possible environment. The Fourth Precept is to practice deep listening, speaking kindly, and understanding others. The Fifth Precept keeps one from consuming toxic materials, prevents addictions to unhelpful activities such as drugs, video games, and violent movies.

Practicing morality and mindfulness in our daily life builds up our awareness of the environment, including self-feeling and mental formations. It helps us to control our actions, speech, and thoughts and prevents damage to the self, others, the environment, and society. At the same time, practicing *sila* protects us from being stuck in the cycles of darkness. It guarantees a bright future with peace and true happiness. In other words, practicing *sila* helps us obtain the mindful energy that gives us wisdom that no one can limit or oppress. Therefore, morality helps us to avoid suffering. It helps us to achieve peace, compassion, and the wisdom to stabilize our lives.

> *"As students of Buddha*
> *To skillfully practice strict ethics*
> *Stay safe in mindfulness*
> *Intelligent and saints all respect."*

12

LOVING SPEECH

"Sometimes practicing saying kind words to others is very simple. All it takes is sitting down for only five to ten minutes with a pure and peaceful mind to observe the breath going in and out. Then, you are able to put on a smile, dispel all suffering, pain, and anger. You are ready to speak calmly and kindly to others from the bottom of the heart."

When you lose the connection with your loved ones, life just feels hard and you can get stuck. If you are unable to listen to others or say kind things to people around you, you'll be lonely and stray helplessly in life, just like sheep having no shepherd to guide them or protect them. Struggles that can't be released nor shared lead to bad moods, contentions, and arguments. You're like a bomb on the inside, ready to explode at any time. None of us wants to be grouchy and reproach our loved ones; yet we're forgetful, continue living without mindfulness, cannot control our own actions, let the anger prey upon us, and pour it on other people, even though we have a lot of precious things to say that could make them feel good. People always say, "Courtesy costs nothing". Through many years of experience in life, our ancestors came up with such a profound yet concise proverb. All you need to do is consider each sentence carefully, ensuring that each word that you're saying to others will make them feel good and pleased. A kind and beautiful word that comes from a warm and loving heart with a respectful manner towards another not only creates a peaceful atmosphere but is also an effective therapy. A right word and a timely action have an incredible ability to bring peace and happiness like a helpful supplement for both your body and soul.

People nowadays are being pulled into materialism. The result of our pursuit of money, material goods, and fame is that we don't have time to look deeply at our lives. You can always buy material things as gifts for your family, but sometimes it's hard to give such appreciation, or even sit down together and open your heart. This is a common tragedy of society nowadays. Lots of families have lost the ability to listen and express love. They suffer in an isolated and cold atmosphere in their own homes. Some people even have to see a psychotherapist to find someone to share with and understand, with the hope of finding a cure for their soul. Therefore, when you love someone and want to be with them, you must learn how to listen, express your love, and say loving words.

LOVING SPEECH

Sometimes practicing saying kind words to others is very simple. All it takes is sitting down for only five to ten minutes with a pure and peaceful mind to observe the breath going in and out. Then, you are able to put on a smile, dispel all suffering, pain, and anger. You are ready to speak calmly and kindly to others from the bottom of the heart. When your mind is filled with anger, annoyance, and insecurity, you can only speak with harshness and bitterness. Losing the ability to say kind and loving words is a terrible barrier that prevents you from making connections with everyone around you and finding your true love and happiness in life.

Bodhisattva Avalokitevara had wisdom and compassion. She vowed to stay in this world to listen and save all mankind from the insecurity, fear, suffering, and desperation in which we are dwelling. Her message was, "Any time you need me, I will be there for you." She is respectfully named *Quan Am*, which means someone with an ability to listen to the calling of sentient beings and understand the suffering of all. Let's follow Bodhisattva Quan Am to observe and practice: "Contemplating the world, listening deeply to surounding sounds, practicing the ultimate principle, practicing right speech, finding means of liberation from greed, anger, and ignorance."[37]

Compassion speech is a magical sound. This is the language that opens the door of love and overcomes problems. It is a soft language, which makes people feel mentally healthy and secure. It brings peace and a cure for your broken soul. The nature of it is mercy.

Contemplated speech means words spoken by an individual who can look deeply into life and listen to the call of every being in this world. This speech diminishes the pain and suffering of all creatures, because it's the voice of someone who truly knows and understands the desperation, pain, and fear of all beings. When you know someone's there for you, the suffering is minimized. Contemplated speech reflects and directly faces life's problems. Its nature is reflecting the truth.

Brahma means noble. It's not an ordinary word but is an elevated one, and it comes from the willingness to bring happiness and take pain away. Infinite view, loving care, satisfaction, and equanimity discharge are the four immeasurable states of consciousness. These are saints' consciousness. If one wants to achieve these four states of mind, he'll have to practice generosity, loving care to others, and removing attachments. God is also love, humaneness, happiness, and justice. If one wants to be connected with God or the Buddha, he will need to practice these four states of mind. If not, entering the Buddha's domicile will be impossible for him no matter how much he prays or talks about the union with Pure Land or Heaven.

Sea tide sound is an authentic word, the speech of truth, and is the teaching of the Buddha. It is a miraculous sound, which can silence wrong thoughts. It's the roar of the lion, which brings the jungle into total silence. This is the sound that changes the world and cures pain.

Liberation sound is incomparable. This word doesn't point to fame, profit, or any other aspects of rivalry. It's the thunder-silence which can dissipate concepts in the mind.

Practicing mindfulness helps you to take a closer step to reach the characteristics of Quan Am Bodhisattva so that love is always there in your heart and opens the door of listening to the truth that surrounds us. Knowing the hurtful consequences of inattentive speech, one should pay attention to his speech, listens to others' suffering, and reduce their pain. Knowing that words bring either happiness or pain to others. We vow only to say things that can build up confidence for others, bring pleasure and hope. We vow to say truthful words that have power of understanding and dispelling problems. We vow not to lie, not to say things that cause conflict or anger. We vow not to proclaim information that we cannot verify, not to criticize or condemn others when things are unsure. We vow not to say things that may cause dispute in a family or an organization.[12]

> *"To practice loving speech to others,*
> *Like sweet juice from Buddha,*
> *Cool off body and mind*
> *Proclaimed wise men."*

13

FILIAL CARE TO PARENTS

"Our parents nurture, shelter, protect, and train us to be helpful to others. They give us unconditional love. Although life has mistreated us, our parents are always the ones to whom we can return to and take refuge"

*P*arents are our blessed ones. The spacious ocean cannot be compared with a mother's care or raising of her child. The sky-high mountain is not comparable to a father's merits. Vietnamese proverbs consider moms as sweet as ba huong bananas, ambrosial sweet rice, or delicious lau sugar cane. Ba hường bananas are very delicious and can be found in the rural areas of Vietnam. How sweet a lau sugar cane is!

When thinking about parents, I think about true love, because no one can ever give out such kind, sweet, and gentle love like a mother and father. There are horrific instances in which parents do the inconceivable and harm their own children, abuse that can be attributed to the abuse inflicted on themselves as a child. However, I still believe that naturally every parent loves their children and would never want their child to suffer. Everyone would like their children to be happy.

In order to gratefully reward parents' efforts, one must live in mindfulness to realize how much time and love parents have devoted to provide the conditions and quality of life one has. Living in awareness of surroundings and appreciating what the self has gained are the keys for one to have an awakened life. The awakened person has the ability to avoid immature thoughts, like complaining about the conditions he inherited from his parents. Often, children want to escape and run away from their parents, living as abandoned children, until one day they appreciate a donation, a loaf of bread, or a cup of water from a stranger while starving and wandering the streets. Then they realize that their parents would never have let them starve. They are the shelter with endless resources for them to be trained and raised. With their unconditional love, children can always take refuge in their parents.

If one looks deep inside his body, he would ask himself: "Who has created this body? Who has given this to me? What has been given?" With this technique, he will figure out the ones who have given this body are his parents, his ancestors. He is the one who has received it, and the thing that is given is his body. There is an intimate connection between the three elements: donor, receiver, and given objects. These three elements are inside everyone. His body contains genes from ancestors, one generation after another, and he will deliver these qualities to his offspring. Seeing this, one understands right away what he should and shouldn't do to maintain himself, his parents, his grandparents, and even his offspring.

Buddhism values filial care and respect for parents. The Buddha himself honors his parents and has mercy on every being. Obviously, almost all sutras and Buddhism books praise filial care, regardless of whether they are from different groups of Buddhism practice. In Pali, *mātā pitu upaṭṭhānaṃ*, means "honoring the parents." Chinese translation: One who is pious will have a chance to take care of his parents.[38] Buddha often said to his disciples, and holy listeners: "The Blessed One has achieved his Buddha title because of his increasing solubility in many cycles of his lives. All credit goes to his parents. Therefore, if one wants to practice Buddhism, he must have the qualifications of providing filial care to his parents." Buddha also emphasized: "There are two persons that cannot easily be repaid. Which two? One's mother and father. Even if one should carry about one's mother on one shoulder and one's father on the other, and while doing so should live for a hundred years; and if one should attend to them by anointing them with balms, by massaging, bathing, and rubbing their limbs, and they even void their urine and excrement there, one still would not have done enough for one's parents, nor would one have repaid them."³⁹

The connection between parents and their children is a sacred, respectful, and honorable relationship. As a child, in order to show how grateful he is, "There are five ways in which a son should minister to his mother and father." He should think: "Having been supported by them, I will support them. I will perform their duties for them. I will keep up the family tradition. I will be worthy of my heritage. After my parent's deaths, I will distribute gifts on their behalf. And there are five ways in which the parents, so ministered to by their son as in the eastern tradition, will reciprocate: they will restrain him from evil, support him in doing good, teach him skills, find him a suitable wife and, in due time, hand over his inheritance to him. In this way, the eastern tradition is preserved, bringing peace and freedom from fear." ⁴⁰

The Buddha reprimanded his disciples if they betrayed their parents. Buddhism doctrines of the North and South Practice Goups consider infidelity to parents as one of the five greatest sins. They are called Five hellish deeds.⁴¹ Therefore, filial piety is the basic qualification of wholesomeness and compassion.

If a person does not respect his parents, he cannot treat others with kindness and respect. Filial piety is the top virtue of a person. From it arises the kindness and care for others, for all of mankind. That is how compassion is developed.

One's streams of humanity flow into culture, creating educational replication. In this cultural replication there are no conflicts between individuals because filial love and loyalty have resolved all conflicts. In other words, he who has filial love for his parents understands others, cares for others, and has loyalty and respect for others. It is a central value (from ancient times to the present) that many religions instill in their followers.

> *"He who is honest and filial,*
> *Takes good care of Mom and Dad,*
> *Is right in this life,*
> *Shall enter the sanctuary of the meditative realm."*

14

RAISING CHILDREN

"Raising children is like an art. Sometimes there must be strict discipline, but sometimes soft words are able to wake them up."

Taking care of children is the highest concern of parents. It is a very natural human action. Children are like flowers, fruits of a tree. They are the continuation of parents. Right after a mother gives birth to an infant, the first thing she does is to smile when seeing her baby. She is happy to hear her crying baby at birth. That love is nurtured and developed from one generation to the next. Parental care for children is socially recognized.

In Pali, *puttasangaho,* means caring, nurturing, teaching children. It's easy to understand why the Buddha advised parents to teach their children when they are young. From birth to adolescence, this is the most imporant and impressionable period for children to develop their personalities. Environment and education in youth can guide children's personalities as they mature. At this young age, there are many special changes in both physiology and mentality. Adolescence starts when children enter puberty and ends when they achieve some level of psychological and physiological maturity. [42]

Teenagers have strong vitality, but at the same time they are vunerable to becoming imbalanced. They are no longer childrren, but they are not yet adults. Their lack of life experience and knowledge are limiting. If they don't get help and education properly from parents, they can easily fall into evil social traps. Westerners say: "monkey see, monkey do". A child is like a monkey. What they see is what they do. Children's behaviors reflect the environment they live in. Their personalities depend on their families' education. At this age, children need to be trained and guided into good manners and morality.

People think that children do not pay attention to serious problems, such as spats between adults, killing animals, or death in general. Instead, when observing an animal be killed, or a death caused by car crash, children do pay attention and reflect on these serious topics. With special regard to topics related to human life, children are full of questions and earnestly desire to understand the world around them. These are the engines for research and study. It is the same if someone pays attention to all beings in this world, such as the purpose of a being's life, he will have a clear mind, with more understanding of the needs in the world and more creativity.

Some parents are listless in their roles in teaching their children. These actions lead to failure in training children. Some parents are very demanding. They impose upon their chidren negative behaviors and treat them unfairly. In reality, at their age, children lack life experience so they temporarily obey their parents. However, it does not mean that they aren't concerned about what is right or wrong. In order to train a child well, it is important for one to be aware of the role and mission to fulfill the function of a parent. In other words, parents must show responsible concern-for the child, not turn themselves into negative role models. Not only does a child need to know right from wrong, what he needs to do and what not, but he also needs the warmth of true love, and encouragement to overcome the fear he faces in life.

Parenting plays a negative role when parents impose upon their children what the parents want them to do without explaining to the children what is right from wrong. For example, parents want to prevent children from playing video games. Instead of showing kids the trauma of video games, they forbid them from updating their knowledge and exposing themselves to advanced technologies. Such parenting is overly controlling. It prevents children from exploring the world and new technologies.

Living on happiness

In some families, the parenting role lasts longer than it should. Even though children are grown up, graduated from college, and have jobs and families of their own, they are still controlled by their parents. Parents should not interfere in their children's lives when they are capable of making decisions themselves. Children need to make decisions and even mistakes to grow up. Over-control of children in this way may cause bad relationships in families. This problem is tragic for many families nowadays.

Some parents believe over-parenting naturely comes from love and care for their children. Instead, they are selfish and interested in the images of their parental roles. By over controlling, people demonstrate egoistic, self-reinforcing and self-serving concerns. "I want you to achieve what I never achieved; I want you to be somebody in the eyes of the world, so that I too can be somebody through you. Don't disappoint me. I sacrificed so much for you. My disapproval of you is intended to make you feel so guilty and uncomfortable that you finally conform to my wishes. And it goes without saying that I know what's best for you. I love you and I will continue to love you if you do what I know is right for you."[43] These questionable motives will be cleared out when one practices mindfulness. He will realize it is selfish, foolish, and mad if he forces his child to be a slave to his dream.

In today's society, people don't seem to pay much attention to the self's natural qualities such as sincerity, compassion, kindness, tolerance, and the ability to forgive.

These traits can be obtained easily if practiced at a young age. In Buddhist scriptures, the Buddha often included interesting stories to educate children. There was a story about honest seven-year-old Rahula, the only son of Siddhartha and Yasodhara. The story took place when the Buddha taught Rahula (his son) not to lie to others.[44] The Buddha pointed to a soaking basin after washing his feet. He asked:

"Rahula, do you see this little amount of water left in the water vessel?

Yes, The Buddha

Even such a little amount, Rahula, is the hermitage of those who are not ashamed to tell a deliberate lie.

Then the Buddha threw away the little water that was left and asked Rahula: Rahula, do you see that little amount of water that was thrown away?

Yes, the Buddha

Even so, Rahula, those who are not ashamed to tell a deliberate lie have thrown away their hermitage.

Then the Buddha turned the water vessel upside down and asked Rahula:

Rahula, do you see this water vessel turned upside down?

Yes, the Buddha

Even so, Rahula, those who are not ashamed to tell a deliberate lie have turned their hermitage upside down.

Then the Buddha turned the water vessel right way up again and asked Rahula: Rahula, do you see this hollow, empty water vessel?

Yes, The Buddha

Even so hollow and empty, Rahula, is the hermitage of those who are not ashamed to tell a deliberate lie."

Authoritarian education intended to blame or scold is just imposing negativity on a child without a good result. Education for children is an art. Strict discipline helps, but sometimes soft talk will get the best result.

Another time, the Buddha taught Rahula how to comtemplate his own actions. He pointed to a mirror and asked Rahula:

"Dear Rahula? What is the purpose of a mirror?

For the purpose of reflection, The Buddha

So too, Rahula, an action with the body should be done after repeated reflection; an action by speech should be done after repeated reflection; an action by mind should be done after repeated reflection." [45]

The teachings are simple, but understandable for young people. The pure innocent mind is sown with the seeds of mindful awareness as a lifestyle of young people.

Parental behavior greatly influences the moral development of children. If parents show that their discipline guides their children toward good pratices in life, then children become more honest with their parents. The Buddha also taught us to review every action afterward: If the action causes harm, you need to consult a wise person and show modesty. He will help you to avoid the same mistake in the future.

Youth is an age when education is viewed as a pattern to shape children's future. Knowledge about the basis of life (and the intimate relationship between people and the universe) is very important for youths.

The following story is recorded in Buddhist literature.[46] While walking in meditation under a tree, Rahula sat down by the Buddha, who picked a leaf and told Rahula: "Do you know where this leaf comes from? This exists because soil, water, and air give nutrients to the tree; heat from the sun make the leaves green. Therefore, this does not exist if other conditions don't exist. Similarly, this body is not me. It's not mine and not my self-notion. People suffer because they have incorrect perceptions about their bodies. They think that the thought, action, and consciousness of their bodies are theirs. Then they act upon ideas to build more 'self', 'myself', and 'mine'. That is a mistake!"

We have forgotten this way of education. Many parents love their children, do everything for them to make them happy, and satisfy their material needs. They only teach children about *what they should get*, but forget to teach them about *caring for and sharing with others*. That teaching will lead to selfishness and ego, which are the sources of suffering. Instead, teaching children persistence, patience, humility, and practicing mindfulness will help them to accept the world more easily. This is like the earth, which accepts everything poured onto it. The earth does not feel bothered about anything. Therefore, if one practices being awake like the earth, he will not be bothered by compliments or reprobations in life.

Today, some schools in advanced countries around the world have seen the benefits of practicing mindful meditation. They apply this program to their students. Too much homework is one of the leading causes of stress, which causes children to be easily angered or get into fights with friends. Practicing mindful meditation will help children regain balance, feel good about themselves, and be comfortable with everyone around them. There are many young people who practice meditation to calm their minds and find peace in the challenges of adolescence. Obviously, meditative focus on breathing is not only beneficial for teenagers, but also helps throughout life's journeys. The value of mindful meditation helps one to return to the present moment and have happiness in the here and now.

It is important to tell a child that life is not simple. In order to achieve something in life, one must have courage when facing difficulties, and have strong will. These are qualities of a successful person which should be instilled in children.

Nowadays, people seem to focus on individualism and weigh the sole thought even if it's against human values, traditions, or good-standing cultural values. Furthermore, it is dangerous for people to get information only through the internet, Facebook, Twitter, and television networks. When these media become the only source of inspiration, it is bad news. The most popular subjects in social networks are masses such as criminals, looters, riots, or acts that drive peope to hatred, or fame. Rarely are there any programs that bring education about humanity. When children have too much exposure to these negative media, negative thoughts and acts of violence are triggered. They lose their true qualities and self-confidence.

There are many benevolent hearts in this world. They are dedicated people who care for others who are sick, those who are homeless, gravely ill children, and frail elderly people, without expecting anything in return. In the depths of human beings are beautiful qualities of compassion and forgiveness. No one wants to steal, kill, exploit, rape, lie, or cause suffering to others. Parents need to guide their children to a good way to develop these beautiful qualities. If a child is trained properly, good qualities are developed, and his future is bright. On the other hand, if the same child is neglected, not taught the right things, and is instead exposed to violent media, he will lose his faith in life and in himself. That is the path of darkness.

Compassion in thoughts and actions bring good health and spirits. In contrast, agressive actions, rude words, and hatred create negative environments around that person. Eventually, he will be attracted by death and crime because of messages from the media. Sometimes, people are exhausted by bad news, but they are unable to stop listening. The danger is that they are deceived and begin losing faith in people and society.

It is important to teach young children about recognizing their own qualities and building self-confidence. Parents are responsible for inspiring children to identify their gifted skills and cultivate them. This practice is like choosing the good seeds and cultivating them. It helps children not only to gain success in the present but also builds self-trust. This way, when grown up, they are independent and can successfully stand on their own feet despite many hardships in life.

I have met students who did not have any idea about their future careers. They did not know what their gifted skills were, and even which major they should take. They tried one major, failed, and then dropped out. They chose another one and again dropped out. Finally, discouraged and having dropped everything, they thought there was nothing for them to pursue.

115
RAISING CHILDREN

Lack of proper care or inadequacy of parents makes it easy for children to fall into such a deadlock. Without difficulties, there is no success. One should never hope that the difficulties will magically disappear and that success will be manifested as a miracle. Look deep into the self; reflect on all capabilities; and pay attention to the skills that fit one's aptitude, interests, passion, and circumstances to choose the most fitting career. Once the career is chosen, one must try hard to maintain progress to achieve the goal. Focusing all of one's available energy to constantly learn and gain confidence to overcome obstacles is the strategy to success. "No pain, no gain". There is no success without barriers and obstacles.

> *"To raising children*
> *Knowing how to live in Dharma joy*
> *Right in this world*
> *Enjoy peaceful life."*

15

SPOUSAL LOVE AND CARE

"True love requires affection and care for each other, as well as mutual understanding, and has the greatest impact on children. Given such positive influence, kids tend to become kind people when they grow up."

To successfully maintain a marriage, both the husband and the wife must take responsibility to care for each other. This is important for the family because a healthy marriage brings peace and joy to all members. Since families are the foundation of society, domestic harmony is crucial for the community at large. Indeed, a happy family and its generated values nourish and direct kids to become stable and successful in the future. Otherwise, if parents fight and disrespect each other on a regular basis, not only they themselves suffer but also their children's lives could be damaged. The negative behavioral pattern from parents tends to be picked up by children, and hence it can be repeated in later generations. On the contrary, if a married couple treats each other well, their children tend to flourish. Therefore, let us practice the Buddhist teachings of love, respect, understanding, and positive speech for the sake of happy marriage and the future of children as well.

Seeking the equivalent phrase of *spousal love and care* in the Pali language, we find *Saṅgah dārassa*. *Saṅgah* means taking care of, and *dārassa* means wife. The phrase specifically describes the caring action of a husband for his wife, though in reality, a couple should reciprocate affection.

An example of spousal love and care can be found in a Vietnamese tradition during feudal times. In one particular example of romance, a married couple worked hard to build a bright future together. Although they took separate roles, both were completely devoted. The husband was immersed in his studies. He burned the midnight oil hoping to win the annual contest organized by the King. Should he win the exam, he would be granted a prestigious title working for the royal government. This would bring honor and wealth to the whole family. On the other hand, the wife also worked day and night, running her small business to support the husband's cause and to raise the children. The day the husband won the contest should be her glory day as well. She would be carried on an honorable hammock, following him on his trip to the kingdom for his inauguration.

Living on happiness

The glory came as a result of spousal love and care. It was a dream of many women. The traditional romance was also pursued by many men. However, not all contestants became the winner. Not all of the hard-working wives were fairly rewarded. Tu Xuong, a famous poet in Vietnam, won the contest at the age of thirty-seven after seven previous failures. To respect his wife's hard work in supporting his cause, Tu wrote:

> *"For long years she worked very hard*
> *Feeding five kids and one grown man*
> *On the winter water, she floated her skinny boat*
> *All by herself like a lone swan*
> *Despite the rain and the scorching sun*
> *Making a living for her nest as a mother bird*
> *While her husband was being a useless swan."*

Nowadays, women's rights of equality are more widely recognized. Although the story does not overcome the historical gender bias, it still sets a good example of spousal love and care: to devote ourselves to our loved ones.

By the same token, the Buddha also touched on the subject of love and marriage. His teaching is aimed at building a happy family. Whoever dreams to have a successful marriage and to raise great kids should learn the Buddhist teaching of spousal love and care. Diligently practicing this will bring the rewards of domestic love, peace and joy. This has a great impact on children. The married couple's affection for each other sets a good example for kids to follow. Their children tend to become happy and kind people when they grow up. Having first started with the married couple, happiness spreads to the whole family, and from one family to another. The ongoing chain reaction builds up a strong society.

The Buddha also addressed love and marriage, in the interest of supporting a peaceful family. The Buddhist teaching of spousal love and care supports the goals of successful relationships and parenting. Diligent practice will bring the rewards of domestic love, peace and joy. The couple's affection and respect for each other sets a positive example for their children and for others, creating a chain reaction contributing to a more peaceful society.

In reality, our society still has many problematic issues despite all of our advanced technology. Heavily preoccupied by materialism, we tend to lose our sense of mutual respect. This is a downward spiral to suffering. At some point, we wonder: Does modern technology make a mistake? Before coming up with an answer, let us examine the major differences between life in non-urban areas and life in big cities.

In some rural areas of Vietnam, people live peacefully in small villages surrounded by trees, rivers, jungles and mountains. In the absence of modern technology, villagers use buffalos to plow rice fields. The economy is slow yet there is no sign of drug abuse, theft, or other crimes. People are happy with life the way it is: slow, simple and happy. This is the opposite of life in the metropolitan cities such as New York, Los Angeles, Paris, Tokyo, London, etc. Although the economy and educational systems are advanced there, crime and divorce rates are outrageously high. People are swamped with work all day long. Hence, living there creates extremely high stress levels.

Observing the villagers' freedom from urban issues, many come to the conviction that modern technology is the culprit of misery. On the other hand, everyone relies on technology for housing, transportation, communication, and medicine. Despising the necessity of technology in hopes of eliminating social problems is impractical. At the same time, social problems could be reduced by working from the root level: Family. Spousal love and care can bring familial love, peace and joy. Such a healthy environment eventually produces brilliant members of society. The social problems will be greatly improved. In that regard, science and technology should still prevail regardless of any issue they might cause.

Also intertwined with the exponentially developing technology, social constructs such as education and economy are rapidly growing. However, one construct tends to be left behind: Spiritual values. In order to achieve peace and happiness, one must develop ethics and morals in tandem with the material aspects of life. Indeed, if we produce tremendous wealth in the world, we must learn how to live in harmony with each other. There must be more development of disciplines such as religions, codes of ethics, laws, rules and regulations to cope with the overwhelming materialism. Emphasis on spiritual values should balance out the obsession with success and money, assuring a healthy growth for society.

Understanding the importance of spiritual values in the modern age, we are inclined to be pro-ethical. Nevertheless, leaving the responsibility upon educators and religious leaders takes away a fundamental resource: family. In fact, family is like a chemical reactor where elementary values are generated. If the five Buddhist precepts (or spousal love and care in particular) are practiced, domestic love, peace and joy will follow. Good values such as respect, honesty, kindness and forgiveness will be generated. The world will be a better place if married couples set an example of love in the family.

Primarily, spousal love and care is conditioned upon one key aspect: Mutual respect. While respect is basic for sustaining any sort of relationship, it is more highly demanded in a marriage. That is because to sustain love, the married couple must feel highly regarded by one another. Indeed, married couples in Asian cultures are known to treat each other like important guests. They take responsibility to care for each other, and their marriage is stable for a long time. By the same token, it is advisable for a couple to get to know each other before getting married. The probation period assures the compatibility of life partners who share most ideology and values. The sharing of values is the most vital aspect of a marriage.

Only if people share the same values can they have mutual respect, which is a vital ingredient for love and affection.

Additionally, spousal love and care take the courage of understanding, accepting, forgiving and being patient. Love is a meaningful concept. In love, we not only admire the strength but also embrace the weakness of the person. Otherwise the feeling is only a selfish sensation. Like how we love chocolate; we crave its creamy sweetness, hoping for a bite to satisfy our appetite. That is not true love. The "L" word is misused, and instant gratification is overstated. Similarly, the desire for beauty and sex is not true love either. A marriage based on lust for beauty and money alone is not stable. Like the instant gratification of chocolate, lust quickly comes and goes. A breakup, therefore, is waiting down the line. Otherwise, with understanding, acceptance, forgiveness and patience, the relationship will endure. Only true love has the power to transform hardship into hope, and only true love is capable of bringing happiness.

Ideally the couple should have support from all around for their marriage. This is because spousal romance is not always rosy. In the beginning, the power of love seems invincible. Yet through time, hearts might be challenged by the complexity of life. This is when a married couple needs support from families, friends, and even counselors. Also, shared ideologies and purposes tend to hold them together. Ultimately, spiritual values give them the guidelines to ride the waves of hardship and strive for happiness. Therefore, married couples should be open to support, reaching out to community as well as seeking spiritualism.

In Buddhist tradition, the bride and the groom take five oaths during their wedding. The ritual is aimed for the newly-weds to take on great spiritual values as they start their new life together:

1. We are aware that all generations of our ancestors and all future generations are present in us.

2. We are aware of the expectations that our ancestors, our children, and their children have of us.

3. We are aware that our joy, peace, freedom, and harmony are the joy, peace, freedom, and harmony of our ancestors, our children, and their children.

4. We are aware that understanding is the very foundation of love.

5. We are aware that blaming and arguing can never help us and only create a wider gap between us; that only understanding, trust, and love can help us change and grow.[47]

These five features of awareness are repeated every month to remind couples and support their relationships to be stronger and happier. The most important consideration is to build a long-lasting relationship for a couple so that their children have a reliable shelter and environment in which to grow up. A happy family not only gives care, and reacts gently toward family members, but all members in turn show their care and treat everyone with respect in society. This reflects the kindness of their family. In addition, when the children grow up they will keep traditional values in their families and transfer those values to their offspring.

One day in San Diego, I attended a class of a psychology professor who helped young couples preparing for marriages. He advised the young men to allow themselves to marry two women at the same time. The young men were amused by the strange advice. He explained that "two women" meant the two sides of the same women (of their prospective wives). One is very kind, understanding, docile, and respectable. On the other hand, she is angry, jealous, and unkind. He continued, if one wants to seek long-term happiness, he must accept both women at the same time. Similarly, young women must marry the two sides of the same man. He is brave, manly, romantic, enthusiastic, honest, thoughtful, and generous. At the same time, he has his weaknesses. Everybody has good and bad sides. Therefore, in order to make a long-term relationship with someone, one must be aware of and accept both sides of the other.

Besides acceptance, caring for each other is equally important. Husband and wife aim to please each other. This affection must be reciprocated. Otherwise, one-way love or lack of affection will lead to dissatisfaction, separation, and divorce. Worst of all, their children, if they have any, can be traumatized from the familial drama.

There are high divorce rates in some western countries, as high as fifty to sixty percent. Some of the main reasons for divorce are a lack of preparatory steps before marriage and education about each party's responsibilities. Each divorce not only causes damage to a couple's lives but also their children's. They grow up without the loving care of either mom or dad (or both).

Last but not least, deliberating over marriage beforehand is necessary. The mental processes during the dating period (such as getting to know the lover, the evaluation of the relationship and learning about marriage) provide a stable foundation for the union. Considering the high divorce rate, these preparatory steps are crucial. Also, because young children are vulnerable to trauma caused by a divorce, deliberation about marriage is a matter of ethics.

> *"Spousal love and care*
> *Take full responsibility*
> *Whoever practices*
> *Will have love, peace and joy."*

16

TO COMPLETE DUTIES

Emotions take away our free will. Once we control our emotions or negative feelings, we gain time and energy to truly live in the here and now. This way, we will have more positive impact on others and our environment which will brings more joy to our lives.

In order to do great things in the world, one must do well on small things for himself. If one wants to share his great heart with others, he must first understand his own needs and love himself. In other words, he must know himself very well. Knowing oneself is not simple, because thoughts are changing in every moment. The flow of the mind changes like young buds in spring which turn to full green in summer, then turn to yellow in fall, and fall off before winter arrives. In the same manner, one's emotions are non-stop flowing streams. After birth, people change with every breath. The body grows old; thoughts and emotions are always changing without one's consciousness. One could be very shy as a child, but become more confident when they grow up. An individual is different from yesterday and he is definitely not the same as in childhood. However, he is identified as an individual constantly growing and influenced by education and the environment around him.

In Pali, *anakula ca kammanta*[48] means completing our own duty. One is said to complete his duties or has true freedom when he allows himself to escape the limits and worries of time. In busy daily life, people often feel 24 hours a day is not enough. Many of us spend too much time worrying about things that have happened in the past (or things that will happen in the future) but forget to enjoy things in the present. We are chasing dream after dream or regretting mistakes made in the past without seeing what we are doing right now.

All of this does not mean we should not plan for our future. The point is that we should be aware of what we have, make reasonable plans for the future, and give up the frivolous thoughts that take up our precious time. It's obvious that if one is not capable of fulfilling his obligations, he is not able to help others. For example, if one lets emotions control his thoughts twenty-four hours a day, he will have no time left to enjoy his meals and things around him. That is not a wise way to spend our valuable time. Instead, we should focus our thoughts and actions on being aware of the needs of others and the surrounding environment and make proper actions to lend our hand at every moment. That is called practicing mindfulness.

Living on happiness

Completing our duties means we are controlling our actions twenty-four hours a day without the interference of negative feelings. Once free of emotions, we can wisely use our time to get in touch with life. We discover more interesting things in life and are more connected. We won't run away from suffering, but instead recognize its causes and how to resolve it. In addition, we should avoid spending time on or involving ourselves with frivolities or vanities, which do not bring happiness to life. If one knows what to do while he is there, his actions become meaningful. In turn, his meaningful actions motivate him to work harder, be stronger, and be creative. We should not let the past overwhelm our feelings. Instead, let it be a lesson to experience life. The present moment is our true life, and it is the root of our future happiness. If one wants his future to be bright, his dreams to come true, he needs to work hard to achieve the dream at this present moment. Obviously, today's happiness is a promise for a bright future.

Buddha repeated many times during his teachings: "Dear disciples, let you light up the torch to lead your way and step forward, let you improve yourself, correct mistakes, and complete your duties of life." This means one absolutely decides his course of actions and is responsible for them. With that idea in mind, one will see life manifesting its beautiful colors, filled with opportunities to achieve happiness and liberation.

Understanding ourselves gives us insight into life, as well as the interdependent relationship between people and other beings. Humans often feel frail when faced with the vast space and ever-changing impermanence of life. Once we know the operations of the mind, we will be prepared to easily accept the impermanence. This way, we can easily adjust our minds to adapt to the world around us. Especially important is that, when provoked by our loved ones, we do not require them to behave in a particular way, or desire them to be like ourselves. Also, it seems negative emotions stop when one knows how to take care of his inner mind. There is no anxiety about praise or the blame in life. In our daily practices, we sometimes can't completely stop our suffering, but at least we can control our words, thoughts, and actions. It is the way to free ourselves from being controlled by our own emotions.

Therefore, focusing in on our duties is a way to return to our true selves. This means we are aware of everything around us. In order to suppress our evil minds, we must let go of the burden of anxiety, overcoming difficulties by using mindful awareness. We must experience that happiness is a result of resolving suffering. The more we transform problems into peace, the more we accept and treasure the uncertainties of life. Without impermanence, we won't value peace and happiness.

> *"To complete our duties*
> *We can see our true minds*
> *Let go of all worries and burdens*
> *Let our minds fly."*

17

GIVING WITH LOVE

"The giving that comes from love, with a great heart, a genuine heart, and the notion of the distinction between the donor and the recipient is no longer present, the fruit of this act will be thousands of times larger than the giving with the intention of just wanting to be known."

Society has always praised the beautiful heart, praising human love and support. Giving love is a meaningful act, also a basic practice to develop compassion and kindness. Usually when you give, it is due to need, so you provide; and the more valuable the object, then the greater the blessings from the giving will be. Of course, there is giving, then there is blessing. Here, what we want to learn is the right way of giving, which involves not only merit but also wisdom.

From pali, *dānā* means giving out, dealing out, almsgiving, liberality, munificence, leniency, beneficence, offering, donation, generosity. In these words, generosity means kindness, which is true of most of the meanings of the word *dānā*. *Dānā* carries a very beautiful and profound content, but sometimes is abused and becomes distorted. Giving is a donation with love and understanding; the person who practices bodhisattva acts will know how to give in the right way. Starting with the mind that wants to help others is a good deed, but to bring all your material possessions to them to have well-known fame, or with the intention of giving to others, or forced giving, is not. This thinking in the word of the Buddha is called impure giving, which is not bright, not beautiful, and not pure.

Many times the Buddha suggests a beautiful act of giving: "When a bodhisattva practices generosity, he does not rely on any object, any form, sound, smell, taste, tactile object, or dharma to practice generosity. That, Subhuti is the spirit in which a bodhisattva practices generosity, not relying on signs. Why? If a bodhisattva practices generosity without relying on signs, the happiness that results cannot be conceived of or measured."[49] In another sutra, the Buddha said, "Generosity is for great benefit we must donate; To reach pure mind, peace and liberation we must donate; Such as fresh flowers, beautiful fragrance. Mindful giving is pure as well, the blessing is in the fullness; If the mind is not pure, then the light is thin; If giving alms with a pure mind then there is extra light. This act of generosity, though it has existed for tens of thousands of years, never disappears."[50] When devotion comes from compassion, with a great and genuine heart, the notion of the distinction between the donor and the recipient is no longer there, then the fruit of this act will be thousands of times larger than the act of giving that is driven by the notion of wanting everyone to know.

To carry the full spirit of donation must mean there is no donor, no recipient, and no gift, and the act constantly rotated and continued; This is called giving with its three pure spheres, and practitioners mindfully observe the giver, receiver, and gift with right awareness, as being like space. You have the idea that the giving must be performed in the right way and to the right person, but in the spirit of giving, there is no donating, no receiving, and no gift. That is, when the mind is willing to donate, then give; we do not care about who the receiver is, what the donation is, or material gift or dharma gift, etc... Therefore, in order to attain the spirituality of the three pure spheres, you need to change the way of thinking about the practicing of the Buddha's teachings. Instead of thinking about ourselves, we should think about other people and always think of how we can help them with our ability and talent. People who have a compassionate heart always place the spirit of service above all else, sometimes without thinking of who is the one to receive the help. When giving with a heart of joy, there is a lot of fun and happiness.

Giving with a pure and sincere heart and with love creates a beautiful and gentle world. It should be said, "Giving is the pure land of the great beings."[51] A Pure

Land is a world of compassion, knowledge, and wisdom, with the light of peace and sweet fruit fragrance. The bodhisattva always carries life aspirations, devoted by the vow and the power of the mind for life.

Funding for almsgiving can be material goods, sometimes love, tolerance, wisdom, or willpower of a great hero. There are many ways of giving. In general, there are three types.

Giving of material objects such as flesh, food, meat, prey, gift, etc., is your attempt to reduce the suffering of people in material terms, through the means of daily living. To understand a broader meaning, donate funds to help develop the economy, distribute welfare and social justice, reconstruct the difficulties caused by natural disasters or social inequality. Life is always different between the rich and the poor where there are natural disasters, so it is very necessary to love, and share donations in life.

Giving of spiritual gifts is your effort s to clear the deadlock, to break the walls of confusion and eliminate the wrong knowledge of humans. This giving is not only teaching the basics of individualism, community, and social life with knowledge such as health, education, psychology, philosophy, law, and politics, but also provides a methodology and practice to reduce suffering in human life. Lacking knowledge and being without a career are some of the reasons leading to human poverty. However, suffering of mind is the most worrisome of all concerns. Teaching the dharma to others can remove their suffering, resolve their spiritual problems and lead them to enlightenment and liberation. The spiritual gift is among the various offerings of the Buddhas, the offering of the Dharma is the highest because it enables the audience to transcend Birth and Death and ultimately attain enlightenment.

Giving a gift of fearlessness is your determination to support, protect and cover for others so they are in peace and can live with less concern and fear. The presence of a person who makes you no longer feel lonely or anxious produces an extremely happy feeling. People face a lot of fear in life. Young children are afraid of parents scolding if they do the wrong thing. When going to school they are afraid of teachers if they do not complete their classwork. In adulthood, we are afraid of not having a job and afraid of lacking career titles. When old, we are afraid of sickness, illness, and having no one beside us to take care of us and provide comfort. Not to mention the fear of war, natural disasters, terrorism, robbery, and the layers and layers of social evils piled up on us.

It is not just the poor who fear, but the rich also have these fears. Practicing the giving of fearlessness is practicing Buddha's teachings to have the right view and clear understanding of all phenomena in the world as impermanent in natural law, therefore, being no longer afraid of natural and environmental changes. When there is body, then there is disease, which is a fact that everyone must face, so they should not be worried when visiting the doctor or when they are in the hospital. The mind is firm on any compliment or loss of life. Not just that you are only happy, but that you can also help others let go of their fear.

People in contemporary society are afraid of illness, so they think that they should eat a lot of healthy food, they should listen to the advertisements that say this food is good for the liver, this food is good for the stomach, and so they eat more than their body needs. In the United States, people seem to depend on medicine, not just the patient taking the medicine, but others who are not sick also take drugs, because they are afraid of disease. Sometimes by taking this medication to cure a disease another medical problem arises.

As such, the gift of fearlessness needs a brave heart and enthusiasm to overcome the great fear in life. To be able to give a spiritual gift requires broader academic wisdom, great knowledge, and wisdom to declare deadlock, guiding everyone on the path to pass on the passion in life. And to be able to give material gifts requires love and a compassionate heart to help with the most misfortune. However, there is a little difference in the practice of these methods of giving, as they are basically derived from true love, from the concept of serving, from careful awareness, and an attitude of openness, from being humble and bowing into life to help people alleviate their suffering.

The Buddha praises those who practice the alms; "Dear children, there are these five benefits of giving. What five? (1) One is dear and agreeable to many people. (2) Good persons resort to one. (3) One acquires a good reputation. (4) One is not deficient in the layperson's duties. (5) With the breakup of the body, after death, one is reborn in a good destination, in a heavenly world. These are the five benefits of giving." [52]

Research by psychologists shows that people with a happy life provide much help, and the more alms they give, the greater the happiness. Happiness and giving are mutually positive. Giving brings more happiness and more happiness brings more giving.

> *"Giving by loving-kindness*
> *With a mind of light and stillness*
> *Spread happiness through all*
> *Bodhicitta seed's bloom is wonderful."*

18

LIVING BY THE BUDDHA'S TEACHING

> *"Practicing the Buddha's teachings makes the body healthier and the mind-gentler; then you are following the right method of his teaching. There is a gentle disengagement because the things we learn have the effect of removing and destroying the things we see, hear, and know that are incorrect."*

The goal of life is to find peace from the material to the spiritual. That happiness is something you create; there is no secret or mystery. How to be happy? How to keep the happiness that you currently have? You know the Buddhist teachings are not based on blessing or wishing. The heart of Buddhism is the Four conferred truths: Buddha said, "Dear friend, both formerly and now, what I teach is suffering and the cessation of suffering."[53] We should see this statement with a very insightful vision which requires the practice of meditation. If you have the study, then the vision is clearer and unraveled.

Living on happiness

From Pali, *dhamma-carivā* means to follow the Dharma practice. It has a correctness of sight which is called the right view. When one sees the truth then the one will engage in right thinking, which is called right thought. The awakening life will help give us the obvious and deeper understanding of the world around us. As such, the practice of Buddhism begins with a sense of mindfulness as a door opens to help us find a correct, bright and profound understanding.

To live by the word of the Buddha means you have clear understanding, a feeling of relief, disengagement, and freshness, rather than feeling dark and heavy. A research article about Buddhism or the Buddha's teaching may make your mind more confused; if you only learn the catechism for the purpose of containing knowledge that is unrelated to the practice of daily life, then you did not learn Buddha's teachings well enough. To practice and live according to the word of the Buddha, if the body is healthier and the mind is gentler, then you are following the right method of the Buddha's teachings.

There is gentle disengagement because the things we learn have the effect of dismantling and destroying the things that we see, hear, and know that are incorrect. There are three original degrees when learning Buddhism. The Study of scriptures is understanding at the level of theory through the word of the Buddha's teachings. Action results from direct application of the doctrine for those of mentally acute ability. Practice based on the teaching of Dharma involves choosing a proper approach to practice. The success of the law is unconceivably perfect or supernormal abilities over the powers of the body and of the mind. We must have clear understanding and dedicate ourselves to practicing Buddha's teachings so that we can have peace, liberation, and freedom.

There are many people who have studied Buddhism for many years, but their mind is still restless because they have just learned, not yet practicing and applying it in life. Therefore, there are still the burdens of the evil mind, like anger and delusion. When you are not able to eradicate the clinging and craving then you are still engulfed in misery. When the Buddha was alive, there was a hermit who asked the Buddha:

"Is there ego? The hermit asks
Buddha just looked at him quietly
The hermit continues to ask! Is there no ego?
Buddha is still quiet

Not getting the answer from the Buddha, the hermit is sad! Then he leaves.

Master Amanda asked the Buddha: why did the Buddha did not answer the hermit's questions? And he said, the Teacher taught us there is no ego, so why did the Teacher not tell the hermit there is no ego?

The Buddha answered:

Living on happiness

The hermit came here to search for a theory, he wanted confirmation of the egolessness theory. I did not teach the theory. I only presented the solution of escaping the suffering. If people come to me for the theory or method then it is a mistake. So, when the hermit asked whether he has ego or is egolessness, I only provided silence and gave no answer. The silent message of the Buddha with that remark, was that the hermit did not want to find the practice process, but was looking for doctrine, to confirmation of the ego or egolessness doctrine, both of which are harmful to him. I would rather use silence, no words."

That is the spirit of Buddhism, just like that: teaching people how to learn and how to practice Buddhism but still find themselves being gentle, peaceful, breaking all the bigotry, because bigotry is the source of all suffering. Those who can live just like that are staying true to the words of Buddha's teachings, and peace will be present.

> *"Living according to the word of Buddha*
> *Often takes persistent effort and delligence*
> *One lives like that*
> *Peaceful conduction will be liberated."*

19

HELPING RELATIVES

"Love each other when you can, when you can see each other, while your eyes can still see, when your hands are warm, and when the heart can feel lively. Realize that now and do not wait until you lose them with regret, sorrow, lament... and wish that you realized it then."

Live with your compassionate heart so that you can create peace and share all the best things with those around you with sincere appreciation and affection for a harmonious world. Live deeply and meaningfully to enjoy life, because life is so short, for there is not much time left for slacking.

The Buddha taught, ñātakānañca saṅgaho, which means helping relatives. Relatives are parents, wife, and children, siblings with the same bloodline, which are the people with whom we are the most intimate in the family relations. Far more are our neighbors in our village, in our country, because we all are brothers in one big family.

142
Living on happiness

In the late afternoon, I walked in a park along the lake watching the sunset slowly disappear behind the mountains. I saw the sparkling golden sunlight on the waves spreading over the lake, and people of all races, all skin colors who come from many different cultures living in the city. All were heading towards the setting sun with a sense of freshness as they dispelled the tiredness and as they found balance after a hard day's work.

The birds' singing, the fresh green grass, the life activities are going around lightly, all creating a quiet space for those who are looking for answers about real life, and about a true value of life. In the midst of the noisy, bustling city that has earned such peaceful moments, it is something very rare and valuable to millions of people living without mindfulness, unknowingly breathing, who live but forget that they are alive.

This life is like an ice cream cone, so enjoy before the ice cream melts. You have ice cream in your hand that you do not know how to enjoy, waiting until it melts with extreme regret. Even though you know that life is not easy, sometimes it is difficult, sometimes dealing with people who are very hateful and hurtful, who break your heart, there are also those who love you and treat you very well. Love and hate are the emotions that create you.

Success or failure is the most valuable lesson that will help you to realize your worth. If someone hurts you, takes advantage of your reputation, or betrays you, then you should forgive them because they help you to realize the meaning of truth. On the other hand, if someone loves you sincerely, then you should love them with all your heart, not just because they teach you how to be good, tolerant and giving.

Only love and compassion can neutralize hatred, and this has been the law for thousands of years. It is not only a law with real value now, but also forever. To overcome hatred, and not spread suffering to others, what you can do is to change negative thoughts into happy, tolerant, and open minds. That is how you enter the door of love and expand the deep space of peace.

Living with a selfish, narrow mind, even if you have a lot of money, you are still the poorest one in the world. Compassion for life is the key to happiness in life. The happy person is a person of compassion and always wishes: "May all beings live in security and in peace, beings who are frail or strong, tall or short, big or small, invisible or visible, near or faraway, already born, or yet to be born; May all of them dwell in perfect tranquility. Let no one do harm to anyone. Let no one put the life of anyone in danger. Let no one, out of anger or ill will, wish anyone any harm. Just as a mother loves and protects her only child at the risk of her own life, cultivate boundless love to offer to all living beings in the entire cosmos."[54]

A person today can laugh with you, but tomorrow that person can go somewhere else, and you will not have the opportunity to meet him or her again. How many happy or sad memories only left in nothingness, just the shadow of the memory, just missing in the shadow. Even so, many people live with their loved ones without knowing to cherish, without helping each other when possible, and without loving each other, and then feel regret when losing their loved ones.

Life is impermanent, it changes in every moment, in each beat, so never wait for tomorrow, as there is no tomorrow. Everything is born and lost in a cycle and no one can avoid the established law of life that is impermanence. Love each other when you can, when you can still see each other, when the eyes are still seen, when the hands are warm with blood flow, when the heart can feel life. Why can you not realize that, until you lose the loved ones, then regretting, missing, and wishing ... wishing... that you cherished them?

If you are interested, be joyful, visit, and forgive each other more so your life will be less tired, bitter and sad. Know how to cherish even the small parts of who surrounds you. Life is impermanent, life is short even just to love. The time we have in our whole lives is not really enough, so why waste time hating, feeling jealousy, and opposing each other?

> "The heart is always opening
> Giving Loving-kindness and compassion
> Help with all loved ones
> Life is peaceful and happiness."

20

ACTION WITHOUT DEFECT

"The weak heart is loose or stressed and is the cause of suffering. To create a calm, balanced state of mind is to observe the deepest issues which will solve the most difficult problems."

Every day you should find ways to make one, two, or more people happy, peaceful, and merry. These people may be family members or friends. Make your loved ones happy by giving them a gift. You do not have to give an expensive gift. By just opening your eyes, being mindful, then you can find a meaningful gift immediately. Gentle speech, a friendly smile, a caring gesture, a warm embrace, a tearful eye, are the gifts you always can give without having to spend a lot of money or effort.

Give others a gift, give others joy, that is the meaning of the pali word *Anavajjāni*. *Vajja* means sin, but this is not a crime that will be punished by imprisonment, or severance. *Anavajjani* means no importunate, no criticism, no remarking. On the contrary, we live with a generous heart, treat others with compassion, virtue, and kindness. Mindfulness in words, caution in behavior to avoid trouble and suffering for others are things worth doing. Conflicts with others are of no use at all. When you do not do or say anything that distorts or hurts others, you feel peace in your heart. To nourish daily mindfulness, you should act by mind rather than act by emotions. Because any emotions, if tested with reason, are largely untrue. Believing in feelings, living with emotions wastes a lot of energy, and every day we receive a lot of emotions arising from our own mind and the surrounding environment.

In everyday life, dealing with many emotions, if you know how to identify and handle emotions, you can transform anything with which you are dissatisfied in life; which is the lesson needed to be successful. The more you know how to reconcile with pain, let go of the emotions sooner, the less you will suffer, the more happiness and peace you will have, and the more freedom you will have in life. If you are stubborn, hold on to things that you think are good and do not have ability to let go of lack the ability to listen, and live day and night with these emotions, then you will constantly suffer.

You need to always be prepared psychologically to face difficulties and suffering in life. When faced with hardships, people have the common mentality of wanting to run away by covering them with a certain pleasure, which only works for a short time and then it will collapse. The best method is to find the cause, then gain the strength to overcome and stand up where you just fell. This is your life preservation and existence; the message is to stand up. However, how you stand up to be less hurting, less scratching, less painful, less corrupting is an art that you need to practice with the Buddha's teachings every day.

Every time I fall down, I get up to mature; to progress one step, I step up one step. We can learn a lot from our own experience, especially learn from our failures. Failures are a valuable lesson to help us to correct mistakes and gain the opportunity to succeed in life. Even though we have a dirty and clumsy temperament, we can learn new habits and cultivate them to create peace and happiness in life. Every step of mindfulness, every breath of consciousness is the opportunity to help us to return to the mind, renew your life without being manipulated by old bad habits. Thus, happiness is created by you; no one has the ability to intervene or is competent to give that to you. Suffering is just the same; no one has the right to punish us except ourselves. When we no longer feel sorry for ourselves we are able to be to refresh ourselves, our gestures of action will not and do not defect ourselves and others.

The reason why we keep on hurting ourselves, causing blemishes for others through our own behavior, is because we have not really returned to take care of our mind. An insecure mind and living in forgetfulness causes disruption.

Living on happiness

When there is so much sorrow in the heart, so much suffering can be released, and even if we have controlled it, it will fall out somewhere else. When you are full of resentment, everything around you becomes unsettled, eating poorly, sleeping poorly, because having someone offend us is hard to ignore and forgive. It may seem like an unrealistic truth, but it is us who inflict suffering on ourselves, resulting in our own behavior. Those who offend or hate us do not create as much suffering as the pain we create for ourselves.

There have been many sufferings that have been going on for decades, but so many of us have no capacity to let go of these and continue to bear those seeds in our hearts. We continue to talk about that pain, and each time we talk about it, the dust cloud of ignorance is presented, leaving us living in anger, living in sadness. Thus, if not ourselves, who can improve this?

We are the ones who destroy our health, peace, and happiness, and numb our minds. The cause of this is a lack of mindfulness. If the culprit is clearly known, then finding the answer is no longer difficult. Each person has his own practice of transforming suffering, on the basis of being calm, nourishing mindfulness in all actions, causing the chance of failure to minimize.

When the heart is weak, stress is the cause of suffering. The Buddha often advised to create a calm, balanced state of mind to observe the deepest issues and to solve the most difficult problems. Whatever happens, you must be calm. Calm down first to observe what's going on and what it feels to be like you. Monitor the in and out breath three times, then you should be mindful enough to make logical and certain decisions that do not harm the people around you. Surely everyone is capable of doing this in fullness.

> *"The heart hurried and weak,*
> *It is the causes all suffering.*
> *To keep the mind balanced and equilibrium,*
> *Action and behaves without defect."*

21

FEAR AND AVOID BAD THINGS

"In a consciousness that arises you have a good thought, a good action then your words are only very nice and can bring joy to yourself, and to others. But in that same idea, a bad thought arises, which can harm one's self, causing suffering for others."

The boundary between good and bad is very close. It is like a silk thread, but the difference between good and evil thoughts are very far apart, like black and white, like the distance between oceans or the distance between the moon and the sun. In a concept that arises, if you have a good thought the words come out very well and can bring joy to yourself and to others. In a similar way, an idea that initiates unwholesome thoughts can be harmful to ourselves, also causing suffering to others.

When we start having a wholesome thought, immediately it enters our mind, forms a seed, and is stored in our consciousness. Of course, the seed was carefully hidden, so it never vanishes. Just like when you plant corn seed in the ground, it lies still in the ground waiting for a convenient opportunity to manifest, and the reappearance will be many times stronger.

There is a poet who said: "Algae grow on the legs of the bridge and after a while it will become beautiful." Algae itself is not pretty, however after looking at it for a long time, it can turn into poetry. Algae reminds us of something in the past, at the time when we were young with a lot of memories and mellow thoughts... the rainy day never ends. The old days gradually fade, like a shadow over the night, like algae on the leg of the bridge. Algae comes to our mind with the blue, wet of blurred memories, the old shadow, smile, steps, shapes. Now, the image no longer exists, years and months have passed. When seeing the algae, the memories come back, a sudden induction into poetry. An old street, old way, an old mark of time, covered with algae, only existing in memory.

When people pay attention to someone, the induction of artifact is more intense and faster than with one that we do not know. If you notice someone or love someone, his or her personality is always present in you, and all you have to do is just think of that person, then love immediately transfers to him or her. Likewise, for the person who practices meditation, the acts involving the transmitting of consciousness happen very quickly, and it does not matter whether they are good or unwholesome acts. Since the mind is more or less settled, it has trained to be purified several times. Just as when you draw something on paper which does not have many ink marks on it, your drawing is easy to see. The mind is less agitated, when sowing into it any action, so the replay happens very fast and is stronger and easier to see.

The daily practice of mindfulness involves preventing bad thoughts from arising in the mind. The flow of consciousness is a person walking on thin ice, and below is the abyss; if not careful, the ice will break into the lake. You know that an unwholesome idea can damage your happiness, breakup a relationship, make you frightened of brotherhood, and burn all the merits that you have built up over a long time. If a thought arises that causes suffering, afflictions and anxiety are present, causing the existence of an insecure mind.

Be mindful of every thought to observe and follow the mind. Just the beginning of a thought can contain a whole world, which contains both good and evil. The light of mindfulness will illuminate so you will know what is good and what is bad. Mindfulness enables you to stop bad thoughts before acting, talking, and thinking. Imagine yesterday there was someone who said bad words to you, now you meet again, you want to say bad things back, and when that thought arises, it occurs to you, if you say bad words to him then he must also suffer as you have suffered, which is very sad. It is necessary to be alert to identify bad thoughts. Being mindful will give you the right view of an unwholesome mind, therefore it is scary.

> *"Fear and avoid evil*
> *Protect and guard thoughts*
> *Keep the body away from wrongful acts*
> *See the mysterious blessings."*

22

NOURISHMENT AND HEALING

"In life, we all need to eat; however, we must know how to use the food so it does not ruin our mind and body. If there is no mindfulness while consuming, it can ruin our body and we will be ungrateful to our ancestors and our children/grandchildren."

The body is a spiritual temple in which there are many ancestors in the past and grandchildren in the future. Each of our cells contains many elements of our parents. To love our parents is to love ourselves, and to love ourselves is to love our children. Keeping our body healthy and our mind fresh is to preserve the spiritual temple for our ancestors. What we absorb into the body and mind, these things are also absorbed into our ancestors and future generations.

Many of us have forgotten the spiritual temple. We do not care, get drunk, and become irritated by the stimulants and irresponsibility. Someone said, just drink a glass of alcohol every week, there is nothing terrible that can ruin the body. Although knowing that drinking alcohol in that quantity for decades does not harm anything, that action can negatively affect children and society. Your grandchildren can become addicted to alcohol when they see you drink alcohol every week. To give up that glass means that you show your children, friends, and society that you are responsible for everyone, which is a profound practice, the action of a wise man.

From Pali, *majjavirati* means avoiding narcotic substances, because these intoxicants will cause you to lose your personality and human qualities. In contemporary society, the constitution and the law are promulgated to protect the individual and private life, which encourages many to think that this body is your own, and you have the right to live your own way. Introductory individualism is a necessity for the protection of human life in society. However, when you look at this body you will see, there are parents, ancestors, flowers, grasses, and the universe. This body also belongs to society, contains beings and many other things. When enlightened by such right view, you overcome the persistence, break the self-discipline, and see the intimate relationship between you and all beings.

Buddhist ethics repeatedly remind us, "Aware of the suffering caused by unmindful consumption, I am committed to cultivating good health, both physical and mental, for myself, my family, and my society by practicing mindful eating, drinking, and consuming. I will practice looking deeply into how I consume the Four Kinds of Nutrients, namely edible foods, sense impressions, volition, and consciousness. I am determined not to gamble, or to use alcohol, drugs, or any other products which contain toxins."[55] Practice this not only for yourself, but for many others including your family and descendants. When a mother is pregnant, food and water are consumed in the body and even the mind can affect the fetus directly and indirectly. If the mother is not conscious and mindful to put healthy foods into her body, it can affect the fetus after birth. If you drink a lot of alcohol, harmful toxins will affect the nerves and brain of your body and the baby.

Americans normally say your health depends on what you absorb each day. "You are what you eat." You are the product of what you eat, this is very clear. In life, you need to eat, but must eat food that nurtures the mind and body. If there is no mindfulness while consuming, it can ruin the body and show your ungratefulness to your ancestors and to your future generations.

Doctors often advise you to chew food many times before you put it in your stomach because that will help you digest more easily. Mindfulness while eating means knowing what food or drink contains toxins or not. Eating consciously means being grateful for where food comes from and being happy while eating. Saying the name of each dish that is served and reading the five contemplations[56] before eating are very interesting to children; it is an education in consumption, eating well and nourishing family happiness.

Knowing what foods our body needs and what foods we need to avoid is important. It is important to be careful about consuming so that your body can be healthy and your mind can be clear. In the consumer-based society, there are many kinds of food that are advertised everywhere and producers find all kinds of ways to have it mass produced, resulting in a lower quality. However, not all foods are good and fit with your health. With a lack of mindfulness, many people like food that satisfies their taste but forget about its quality, and how it can cause many illnesses that torment our body. Many of us go out to buy so much food, over eat, and then become overweight, even obese, to then spend money on doctors to lose the weight. It is an impossible disease in our society nowadays.

When we are bored, lonely, and desperate, many of us often turn to alcohol to release our negative emotions and stress. Maybe alcohol can numb our pain momentarily, but in the end, it makes us more afflicted. We drink alcohol to relieve sadness, but the more we drink, the more anxiety, depression, and stress we experience, and the more our personality starts to deteriorate. Many people cannot escape this cycle, immersed in that leads to inevitable suffering. Worse yet, there are too many teenagers who have fallen into the sinful way, gangs, violence, and part of it is caused by alcoholism.

Alcohol abuse threatens to destroy the body, destroy the future, break families, and disorganize social order. Be aware of this because we must find ways to protect ourselves. This message needs to be discussed with care and seriousness because it affects our happiness and our future generations' happiness.

It is necessary for you to have a basic knowledge of the harmful effects of alcohol and take responsibility of your own and acknowledge the problem at hand. If you are one of those who have already become addicted to alcohol, then you must decide to give it up. You should see alcohol as an enemy that can kill your life, instigate conflict, and destroy society.

During a holiday retreat, I heard one western meditator, Aileen Smith, who was very happy in practicing meditation, enjoy the healthy traditional Buddhist culture at the monastery. Aileen was really fed up with drinking alcohol, eating meat, and partying during the holidays. Many people recognize the health risks of alcohol and should think seriously about this issue.

Young people nowadays have to see the vision, which allows us to remind parents to pay particular attention to the spiritual involvement and lifestyle of their children. Often, parents take care of their children's daily physical activities, sometimes giving their children unhealthy things. There are many parents who are unable to transmit the values of spiritual heritage to their children. If parents themselves are also seeking satisfaction in alcohol then how can they have anything left to give to their children?

Someone with no spiritual life or no practice in a solid truth, will believe that the fun of alcohol will be the only solution. When parents and teachers are so poor in spiritual dedication, then the young people do not have a firm support. Meanwhile, young people need to be absorbed, educated, and nourished with a sense of security without having to go through drinking. The work of educators and parents is to help children find spiritual value deep inside them with true peace. However, if parents and teachers do not have it, then how can they show it to the young people?

When we are aware of the harmful effects of alcohol, it is not only for ourselves but also for our children and the next generations. The material that nourishes the soul, can reach the moon, see the light mist, enjoy the spring flower, and see the innocent smile of the baby. Happiness will be present immediately when you practice giving up alcohol, which is something you can do.

> *"Diligence Effortlessly day and night*
> *Nourishment and healing by not using narcotic substances*
> *Free from all sufferings*
> *No sorrow no fear."*

23

DILIGENTLY DO GOOD DEEDS

"When we practice or do something, we need to lead in the right view way, when we achieve good results, we experience joy and good results. Benefit ourselves and everyone around us naturally by having faith to be more diligent."

As human beings, when we were born with endless urges, we want to learn to grow and to survive, and modern civilization has stimulated these impulses to arise more strongly. Rushing to keep up with life is stressful. When the inner world is unstable, external circumstances tend to be unstable, so that your inner peace and freshness can be missed. The more we seek happiness, then happiness and peace are more difficult to grasp, because happiness does not depend on the outside world or modern civilization; happiness is the silence of the soul that is seen in the person who is diligent in practice to find his true self.

161
DILIGENTLY DO GOOD DEEDS

From Pali, we have the word *appamādo*, which is alertness, awareness of presence, presence of mindfulness, watchfulness, vigilance, attention, observation, careful and cautious consideration thereby inevitably leading to thoroughness, meticulousness, enthusiasm, seriousness, diligence, precision, prudence, common sense and good judgment. The *appamādo* is the word that indicates a person of diligence; it is a source of energy that gives you strength in life. This energy must be built on the right view which will create long-lasting happiness. There are many people who are very diligent; they are influenced by undue actions such as talent, identity, benefit, etc., all of which are not conducive to peace and free will. The more entangled the more insecure actions, those are called evil diligence.

Sometimes, although not attracted by fame, appearance, or material things, the heart may contain many insecurities and suffering. We cannot sit still, because when sitting down the pain of suffering appears unbearable. So, we have to find something to do, find something to say, find something to eat to forget our suffering. Due to the inability to face suffering, we have found a job to fill the emptiness of the heart, with the loneliness of hopelessness, the partial closure of insecurity, we work hard on this job or that job, but still we are not a diligent person. When practicing, for many of us, the more we go to pagodas, the more we help people, the more we chant, the more we meditate. However, this follows a practice that is distanced from the real life, away from the people around us. Whether we spend a lot of time practicing or not, this practice should be directed to right view, right thinking, right speech, right action, right livelihood, mindfulness and right concentration.

The Buddha teaches, *appamādo ca dhammesu*, which means "diligently doing good or good things, good deeds having the power to transform suffering and insecurity." Thus, diligence here is nourished and released into the proper parts of the eight paths of transformation that lead to happiness. Right Effort is always coupled and attached to right understanding. When you do work to benefit the masses, there is a spontaneous joy in your heart. When you know the path to practice that leads to true happiness, then your mind starts to dance with joy. The joy and happiness is the energy that motivates you to be more diligent. So, we know when you develop work with compassion, many benefits will go with it. Then we tell ourselves to nurture this job. Or when you come to the spiritual center for meditation for thirty minutes or walking meditation in the park ... all of these will help transform unwholesome minds and reduce stress. So, we have to be determined to learn how to sit and meditate well and apply it in everyday life. Whenever you have anxious seeds, sit down or walk for thirty minutes to keep your mind refreshed, light and healthy.

When we are new to Buddhism, the more we learn, the more we work on the merit, the more we are happy and in peace. However, there are many of us who have known the religion for decades, have gone to the temple every week, heard the master's teachings, listened to the professor speaking every day, but suffering still exists. This may be because we do not know the key to life and do not know the practice clearly. So, when we practice we need help to guide us in the right way, and when we achieve good results, to experience the joy of good results that benefits ourselves and everyone around us. Then naturally we have the confidence to be more diligent.

The word *sammappadhana*, meaning right diligence or right effort, is understood to be the content of the four right efforts. The word *right diligence* has the meaning of hard work and diligence, which is a process of developing our mind in a good way.

1. Because of wanting to get rid of the bad things that were born, work diligently.

2. Because of wanting to cause the unborn bad things not to arise, work diligently.

3. Because of wanting to cause good deeds that have not yet arisen, work diligently.

4. Because of wanting to nurture the good things that have arisen, work diligently.

According to Buddhist psychology, the place in the bottom of the mind is called stored consciousness. Sometimes it called background consciousness. The consciousness that lies ahead is called foreground consciousness. It is a place that is capable of storing seeds that are both good and evil, bad, cute and not cute, tolerant and narrow, forgiving and selfish, ghost and Buddha minds. When an unwholesome seed arises, the seed of the Indolence arises, and it is brought up on the surface of consciousness into the unwholesome mind. Without the intervention of the right understanding and mindfulness, the unwholesome seed stays the same and sometimes it grows bigger and stronger. The negative mind occupies the space of consciousness. It's the kind of love that can hurt you, and can bring up frustration; it leaves the consciousness and backs down to sleep under consciousness. It comes back, turns into the unwholesome seed, and that seed is stored quietly in the bottom of consciousness.

Mindfulness has the power to see that process, so practice the four right efforts to counter and transform the unwholesome seed before it arises and develops. For example, when we have anger, blame, loneliness for no reason, then we know these are not good activities of the mind. When we realize, that in us there are seeds of unwholesome minds, we are angry, then anger is present in us. When we have the ability to simply identify these, then that anger may vanish. The Buddha presented an image: a carpenter wanted to replace a broken wedge kept between one piece of wood and another. The wedge was supposed to stay between the two pieces of wood, which could break at any time without a new wedge. Thus, "Just as a skilled carpenter or his apprentice would use a small peg to knock out, drive out, and pull out a large one; in the same way, if evil, unskillful thoughts, connected with desire, aversion, or delusion, arise in a person while he is referring to and attending to a particular theme, he should attend to another theme, apart from that one, connected with what is skillful."[57]

Practicing or doing anything that brings you peace, relaxation, and lightness is a motivation to help you be more diligent. The more you do good deeds the happier you are in your life and with the people around you. So, practicing good deeds and cultivation is the key to help us to have a lot of love and energy in life.

> *"Try right Diligently to do good deeds*
> *Energetic not tired*
> *It does not matter Reputation and wealth*
> *Perfect the Enlightened one."*

24

HOMAGE IS BEAUTIFUL

"Reverence is born from the heart that promotes compassion, which causes the love from many, the fruit of love, the peace and joy of life."

Reverence is a fundamental virtue of the human being, the foundation for developing generosity and forgiveness for oneself and others. From Pali, we have the word gārava, which is reverence toward, respect for, esteem. Reverence arises from the heart, with a true heart to the Buddha - a full enlightened being; for the Dharma, it has the power to transform and heal suffering; for Sanghas who have cultivated us to practice; for parents; for the nation and the benefactors who have sheltered us in life are a beauty of humanity.

We pay homage to the Buddha (*Buddha Gāravatā*) because he is a human being like us, but he has overcome all the temptations of life and he is always living in awareness; a human being who lives in the world without being bound by fame, wealth, and status; a person who truly understands the world, so peaceful in the midst of life, taking each step in a leisurely pace, smiling with each loss and gain in life. This is a mighty worth to be admired and respected. This winter I stayed in the monastery for three months, a wonderful holiday with the Sanghas on the mountain covered with snow. I was born and raised in a tropical country where there are only two seasons: sunny and rainy. After arriving to the United States, I lived in a similar climate, spending my first few years in the United States under the hot Texas sun. Having never been exposed to snow before, my body was unable to adjust and I got sick easily. During the retreat, twice a day, all practitioners would go to the meditation hall, despite the weather. On one very cold morning, the temperature was minus 10 degrees Celsius. A cold that chilled me to the bones and that blanketed the meditation hall in snow. Trees were bare, stripped of their leafy greens and leaving only a skeleton of stems and branches, drained to fight the cold winter. Sitting in the meditation hall, I recalled the image of the Buddha sitting on the snowy mountains 26 centuries ago, a great man who opened the source of wisdom for humanity. I give respect to the Buddha because he discovered the path of practice so that people may recognize the values, the nature of existence, and the mystery of life. Thousands of years later, many generations have relied on him to live on the path of compassion and wisdom. Thus, the Buddha was called the supreme figure, capable of subduing man, the master of both heaven and earth, the perfect awakened one who is the most venerated of all.

It is an important part of practice to pay homage to the Dharma (*Dhamma gāravatā*). Dhamma here is the teachings of the Buddha, the magic of the Buddha's doctrine, which is recorded in the three sutras. By practicing this doctrine, we will have a capability to transform suffering, and achieve happiness in the present moment. The teachings are worthy at all times, we only need to consistently practice, and there will be peace in practicing, with no need to wait for many decades. The teachings of the Buddha are very practical and you yourself can see it, it is not mysterious, superstitious and fanatical. On the contrary, the teachings have the power to lead us to the sublimation of life, the ability to suppress defilement, anxiety, sadness, to live leisurely, to be refreshed. The teachings have conquered all classes of intellectuals and scientists. Human beings can self-achieve the miracles on their own.

Pay homage to the Sangha (*Sangha gāravatā*), because the Sangha of the Holiness is an organization that is walking on the path of enlightenment and righteousness. The Sangha is practicing the teachings of the Buddha and is proclaiming the truth for all of us to follow the path of the Holiness, to help save people from the wrong path. Living contentedly and with less desire, spending more time studying and meditating is the basic way of life of the Sangha.

Thus, the Sangha of the Buddha is worthy of admiration, reverence, and offering, the most precious blessing in the world. The Buddha, Dharma and Sangha are three precious stones in life. If anyone has the grace to be close to learn and practice, there will be much more happiness and peace in life. The Buddha taught, my dear friend! Those who have respect for the Buddha, the Dharma, and the Sangha will not accidently drift away from the intention, and he is on the path to nibbana.

Pay upmost respect to morals (*Sikkhā gāravatā*). *Sikkha* means to study, train, and discipline, in reference to ethics or precepts. Practice the virtues that you have promised to live up to, because practicing every virtue means you have more freedom, more happiness, and more joy in life. Every day, you hear a lot of tragic stories that have happened. So much suffering is due to the result of alcoholism, drug addiction, sexual abuse, guns, and other social evils which persevere from generation to generation. If humans are not guided by a moral norm to protect themselves, they will gradually fall into violence, fear, hatred, and insecurity and eventually become ill. Respect ethics as a standard of living, and it will lead to a peaceful, healthy, and happy life.

Pay homage to meditation (*Samādhi gāravatā*). There is a Pali word, *samadhi*, which is concentration. When meditation is practiced, the mind is at rest, helping you return to the present moment, recognizing what is going on around you. Mindfulness helps us to be aware of what is going on in our body, the feeling, the mind and the world around us. Mindfulness protects us, our loved ones, our family, society, and promotes peace in the present and the future. Life is only meaningful when we are aware of the present moment, feeling everything around us.

Respect carefulness (*Appamāda gāravatā*). From Pali, *Appamāda* means thoughtfulness, carefulness, conscientiousness, watchfulness, vigilance, earnestness. It means not wasting time on useless things, but on the contrary, being aware of all actions. Mindfulness is the key to help you return to reality, so that you no longer have the idea of pursuing anything other than what you are. The restless mind worries, which motivates us to do things in vain. The most important thing is to have mindfulness, or self-awareness, and self-motivation in doing things. When we are unaware of our motivations when thinking, talking, and acting, and in some cases even when we are aware of the motives, we often defend for them. Thus, mindfulness is a key to help us to return to our body and guide the mind in the same direction. Or to be aware of whatever is taking place in the present without any prejudice. The important thing is to be aware of our own mind, so we will have the opportunity to recognize our thoughts clearly.

Honor hospitality (*Patisanthā gāravatā*). From Pali, we have the word *patisanthata*, which means kindly received.

By meditating, we love others just like we love ourselves and we are able to treat others with a non-discriminating heart. Encourage others to share the joy of life and help people to reduce their pain. Sometimes sharing a meal, a piece of bread, or a story of virtue, is essential in life.

Thus, in honoring the revered one, we can see the values of truth are one of the beauties of human affection. Practicing reverence as a natural part of daily life will bring us true happiness. Revelation is derived from the heart to increase compassion, which causes many people to give the fruit of love, bringing peace and joy to life.

> *"Reverence is the nurturing of our beauty*
> *The grow so many good deeds*
> *To make people respect*
> *Bring joy and peace to life."*

25

PRACTICING TO BE HUMBLE

"If you are humble, polite, and respectful to everyone, you will have true joy and happiness, and wherever you go you will receive kindness and admiration."

Lowliness and humility are very nice virtues, like a lovely flower chain when worn to make us beautiful and fresh. In Pali, Nivāto means lowliness, humility. If we are humble, polite, and respectful of other people, we have true joy and happiness, and wherever we go we will receive love and admiration. Arrogance is the mindset that distinguishes between oneself and others and measures qualities as low, equal or better, which is an attitude that is completely opposite to the heart of humility and politeness.

The more feelings of guilt we have, the greater our suffering. It is a feature of unwholesome minds, and it is a slip in our mind that is hard to see. The mind can be described in the following way: "If you think you are greater, less than, or equal, you cause dissension. When those three complexes have ended, nothing can agitate your mind."[58] Happiness does not thrive in the heart when there is dispute. Disputes can be expressed through actions such as jealousy, discrimination, blame, arrogance, and denigration; arguments only belong to the domain of language.

If you look deeply to see the true nature of the conflicted mind, you will see that they are only thoughts that lead you to the dark and divided paths. With mindfulness, we can clearly see the delusional thoughts, and we will not be pulled by the ego of an arrogant mind, instead having respect, reverence, and humility for everyone.

People are a living entity in the community, so mutual respect is a necessary condition. Our happiness is related to the well-being of the community, and the suffering of the community has both a direct and indirect impact on our lives. If we are looking for happiness by arguing, winning and losing, meaning we are seeking happiness for your ego selves, then we will never find true happiness. People are less happy and lack compassion because of our tendency to divide and seek happiness by looking down on others.

When facing a person whose status, inheritance, career, reputation, or academic status is lower than yours, and you have the idea that he or she is inferior to you in authority, education, luxurious living, intelligence, etc., then you are making unhelpful comparisons and not practicing humility.

Self-conceit comes from the comparative mind, and all of us have these seeds to some extent. These ideas are derived from discriminating between oneself and others, even though we can see that we are human beings, are brothers and sisters living on the same planet, sharing the same conditions and blood, crying the same salty tears, and battling with our own weaknesses. Beauty, such as that of beautiful flowers, contributes to life. In recognizing this, you can break out of arrogance.

When we meet someone with an equal level of knowledge as us, but we think that we are better than that person, the term Buddhists use is *over arrogant*. It is derived from the discriminating mind. Be careful when listening to statements like "all of us are equal." At first it sounds convincing, but in the spirit of this doctrine there is still a distinction in it. Only when we can really see that we and others are the same, then will we know the best truth. If there is someone better than us, better than us in everything, yet we think that we are better than that person; that kind of discriminating mind is over arrogant.

There is a very basic kind of pride, which rises to false perceptions such as a wrong view about form, feeling, perception, action, consciousness. People are often caught up in three notions of "self, mine, and my." So, the Buddha said, "this body is not self, body and self are not one, and body and self are not two different things." We must escape from these ideas. Practice how to take away the idea of self and non-self. When the five skandhas are empty, they take away the notion of self for feeling, for thought, for action, and for awakening. "This body itself is emptiness and emptiness itself is this body. This body is not other than emptiness and emptiness is not other than this body. The same is true of feelings, perceptions, mental formations, and consciousness."[59] You can see that in the five skandhas, there is no self, and the five skandhas are not self. Self is not isolated from the five skandhas. It is not in the five skandhas, and the five skandhas are not in the self.

The exercise of humility is of course still your choice. If that's what you want, then you will be able to do it at any time, for example, from reading this. When your practice begins, you will find humility is a great and valuable lesson. The lesson of humility requires that you try to match such a fight with yourself no more and no less.

> *"To practice humility*
> *Be Liberated from the concept of self*
> *To see all of the five skandhas are equally empty,*
> *no birth and no death of life."*

26

KNOWING ENOUGH IS PEACEFUL

"People living in satisfaction are satisfied with what they have, content with the things around them."

We live in a consumer society, an age of technological development that reaches the pinnacle of science and technology. It is the incessant inventions in technology that make people connect more easily, creating a more modern civilized society. But the strange thing is that everyone agrees that people living in technologically developed countries, abundant in material goods, are less happy, less satisfied, and sometimes more miserable. There is more stress for people in these developed countries than those living in developing countries.

In one of the winter retreats, there was a mother taking her son to practice at the monastery for a week, and after the retreat she asked her son to stay in the monastery for a few months. The mother had said that her son had dropped out of high school, had become corrupt, and had not listened to his parents. The son looked smart, he was strong, and we could see intense vitality within in him. However, the lack of motivation to pursue his studies was caused by lack of family care, as his parents worked seven days a week. That is the consequence of chasing material comforts. There are many people who spend their lives chasing material things, so that they have no time to breathe and no time to eat. They may have a beautiful house but not know how to look after and enjoy what they worked hard for. It does not stop there; Those caught in the vortex of the world that consumes, may suffer countless illnesses such as heart disease, hypertension, high blood pressure, etc. One way that living without proper awareness can occur for people in contemporary society is through unpredictable eating. We need to recognize this so we can stop and care for ourselves, have time for family, be aware of what we have, and enjoy the gift that nature gives us, which is amazing happiness.

In Pali, we have the word *santutthī*, which is satisfaction or contentment. Thus, according to the teachings of the Buddha, human beings should be satisfied with what they have, content with what is around them. When you are aware of what you have, you are not frantically pursuing material things outside, nor stingily destroying yourself. Thus, contentment is not an asceticism as it is imagined by many; it is a nuance, a psychological attitude of an educated and intellectual person. Because complete self-knowledge is not a solid dogma that binds man, it is not about saying how much is enough, or how much is less desire. In other words, living to know enough gives us a balance in life, not to be too passionate, to go crazy with the pleasures of endless human instincts, and also to not be so harsh on ourselves. Consequences of the pursuit of desire are suffering and eradication. On the other hand, self-immolation on the path of wanting to destroy the body is extremism.

In today's society, it is necessary to have the right attitude towards consciousness to escape the insecurity of material life. Many people misunderstand the teachings of life. Knowing enough is about closing the aspirations and dreams of high-class lifestyle. In fact, the psychological focus of living a "just enough" lifestyle is to be free from endless human desires, the desires that will never be satisfied and which are the cause of suffering, insecurity, and loss of the real meaning of life. Being content with what you have is not promoting idleness, encouraging poor living, not saying that if you have a meal then there is no need to do anything. Satisfaction brings enjoyment to life; to enjoy your achievement, to have time to care for yourself, is not an ideal that intentionally encourages you to be content with poverty, or laziness. Buddhism always encourages and respects legitimate desires and aspirations.

Living with little desire for satisfaction is living with awareness of what you have. When wealthy people know how to use their wealth wisely, they avoid living in luxury, and instead spend their wealth and share it with others. Such people are hard to find! Most of them are entangled in the idea of chasing material and are always looking forward to gaining more. Falling into the vortex makes people lose touch with reality and lose happiness, when wealth should theoretically be able to bring true peace.

Desire causes people to often be anxious, spinning, doubting what will happen, always living in insecurity, which can be the cause of mental and emotional illness. Outside, wealthy people are elaborate with their dazzling clothing, material comfort, and seem to have done quite well, but inside their minds there is so much tension and insecurity. At first, they are very friendly, with no problems or complaints, but then later you will hear all of their troubles, concerns and sorrows. Many people express being uncomfortable or dissatisfied with their lives. The feeling of emptiness, the loneliness, the pressure, the atmosphere of turmoil is present in today's consumer world. You can hide unstable feelings from people around you, but you cannot hide them from yourself, so it is very difficult to build a moral and peaceful foundation for life for yourself.

For many people, material comforts will improve physical well-being; therefore modern western countries should be happier than those living in developing country. If you look closely, though, modern advances in material science and technology do not seem to bring much happiness to humans! There are only high-rise buildings, streets, vehicles, and streets crowded with pedestrians. Of course, there is some reduction in suffering from disease and advances in education; however it seems not to be an overall improvement.

Therefore, you need to have the courage to resist the hectic and busy lifestyle of today's society. Living well, simple and minimalist, with minimal consumption, is the key to helping you step out of the disease era. When you experience the peace of a simple life, with knowing enough, you feel much healthier and freer. Happiness or suffering is dependent on how you live your life, and if you know how to control and minimize your consumption, peace will be present.

> *"Desire causes more sorrow*
> *Misery and suffering follow*
> *Knowing just enough then peace*
> *Present happiness body and mind."*

27

HAPPINESS IS GRATEFULNESS

> *"It is obvious that when a person does not know how to be grateful and is ungrateful to his parents, he can hardly be a man who behaves humanely with friends, family and community. Filial piety is clearly the utmost virtue that stands at the forefront of human virtues."*

A tradition of Western culture, Thanksgiving's Day, is a day celebrated nationwide with the intent to give thanks to our family, friends, and fortunes. An action that is practiced daily in Christian followers, who express thanks to God, because they believe that God gave life to men and created the world as we know it. In the Buddhist tradition, gratitude is expressed through four virtues: the grace of parents who have given us birth; virtues of the nuns and the monks who have taught us spiritual life; the grace of good friendship in the companion, helping you in difficulties; the grace of the sentient beings accidentally bringing to you the necessary conditions for life.

The word in Pali is *kataññutā*, which is gratefulness. As the heart is the soul of the life's rhythm, gratitude is the beat in life's rhythm. A sound that is full of human love, and this human love holds the substance of the noble meaning, which symbolizes the beauty of human culture. It is difficult for those who grow up in life lacking the substance of human affection. Not only the Vietnamese, but most cultures praise and appreciate humanity, praise the human love that begins with the love in the family between parents and children. Love has always been in the hearts of the Vietnamese people, creating a beauty of traditional culture. In the experience of real life, this humanity expresses the relationship between people that is justified by love, by the relationship of the biological father called the *Decorum*, by the relationship of neighbors called *Kindness* and *Uprightness*, through relations between the so-called *Faithfulness*. It is this beautiful human love that causes international friendship, and from which love of nature and life are established. When humanity engages in behavior to build social relationships, establish peace and happiness for the families and international communities, it is called moral behavior. The content of true morals is the true love of living and gratitude.

Humankind originates from living people who know gratitude, which is the root of all virtues. Ancient folk literature, as well as modern day intellectual literature, warmly praise filial piety, or the gratitude to parents. The mother has nurtured and cherished her children since birth with all her heart and body, with the kindness and teaching of the father. The Mother has given her children sweet milk with all her love, chewed rice for her children with her heart, given her children every gesture, every encouraging eye, which goes into the pure spirit of the children from childhood. The mother has led her children step by step, taught her children to speak and to read, until they have grown up. Almost all the resources in life for children are from their parents.

A mother's love for her children is so sweet and so deep that the aging mothers are compared to bananas, a kind of sticky rice, and a sweet sugar. I like the way that country people used to describe the soulful rustic mothers by a verse that contains sweet feelings. Aging mothers are like three-flavor bananas, like honey sticky rice, like mild sugar cane. Mothers are always there to comfort you when the life is uncertain, or when the wind becomes fierce; you can feel the warm and imbued sweetness of motherhood, sweet as a fragrant banana, soothing sweet as honey sticky rice, and a deep taste in the throat as sugar cane. A mother's love is forever lasting, and no ink can provide a description.

When I grew up to start my life, when my heart was first moved by life, I started to realize the divine love that my mother gave me. I wrote the verse to remind myself that I have a mother, and to cherish and live up to being my mother's child.

> *Mother is cool moonbeam;*
> *Is fresh flowers is the branches of positive lobes.*
> *Her lullaby for children is the whole paradise;*
> *Gives children all her warm love.*
> *On each of my steps,*
> *I silently remember the image of mother, in every heartbeat,*
> *I wish to live very firmly relaxed and happy.*

The unconditional loving of our parents was deeply felt by poets and lyricists, who sang in profound lyrics, poems that describe the love of mother as the flow of water that never stops, and father's merits to soar as high as the majestic Himalayan mountains. If you are a good child of your father and mother then you will live deep, each step on the path of your life will have your mother's shape, each of your breaths will be imprinted with your dear father's image. I know that there were times when you did not agree with your parents or there were times when you did not want to talk to your parents. You have the right to be angry, have the right to blame them. But do not be naive enough to be disloyal to your mother, because in each cell of your body is your father and mother. You know that no matter what success or failure in your life, the one who stands by your side for congratulating and comforting is none other than your mother, for the mother is divine and gentle.

Motherhood is the root of love; from early childhood your mother taught you about love, an indispensable virtue in life. Without a mother, how can you feel love? So, give thanks to the mother's love. A love that watered the seed, a love that taught you to love nature, a love that gave you that human affection that is craved; and give thanks to your mother so you develop and nurture gracious compassion.

The concept of a mother's feelings covers all nobility and is sacred, so the Vietnamese see filial piety to parents as being equal to all human values. The great poet Nguyen Du talked about filial piety through the character of Thuy Kieu with the choice between the life of being a dutiful daughter to her parents and the promising full happiness of marriage with her lover from the Kim family. Because of her filial piety she decided to sell herself for her father's freedom, a choice which tells us that our tradition puts weight upon human love, motherhood. "As she hedged virginity, dust to murkiness would she lent?" (Story of Kieu). Kieu's filial mind is the most outstanding feature in Nguyen Du's story. Kieu's heart is like a message filled with human material, respected by everyone, and the dust of her bitter years never fades.

The Buddha taught us to be good, compassionate, generous, forgiving, tolerant, always taking filial piety and humanity as the foundation for building a happy family life, good community and peace in the process of liberation. Therefore, Buddhism is easily integrated into human life everywhere and accepted as a way to live a meaningful life. So, it is obvious, as you see the classic literature in Buddhism praising filial piety. The Buddha often teaches his disciples: I have experienced many recent efforts to become a Buddha, all with the gratitude of parents. So, you are human beings and cannot be disloyal to your parents.

The Buddha also taught: "As a filial child, having the opportunity to support your parents, you should take care of the family, keep the house in peace, not to fall into poverty, which is the biggest auspicious task." He always encourages you to be kind to your parents, because those who can do that are close to the Buddha and like to respect the Buddha. He reprimanded anyone who was not filial to his parents. The tradition of Theravada and Mahayana classify being unfilial to parents as a felony which is one of five greatest sins in the world, from which one cannot be rescued. Thus, filial piety is the moral foundation of human beings, the basic spirituality, from which clear states of mind and liberation are developed.

It is obvious that when a person does not know how to be grateful and is disloyal to his parents, it is hard for him to be a man who treats his friends, family and community humanly. Filial piety is clearly the virtue that stands at the forefront of human virtues. From filial piety, humanity is educated and nurtured. Thanks to gratitude, human beings have emotion before the suffering and loss of humanity and are the seeds of happiness in present and future life.

This stream of human love flows into the cultural field creating a healthy environment and flowing into the education that creates human knowledge. In this environment, people live together in harmony and compassion, without fighting for power, giving protection to each other without the idea of eliminating each other. In human culture, there is no contradiction within filial piety, compassion, tolerance and grace, because the essence of these qualities is for the sake of a noble character. When you have a filial heart, you can accept, tolerate, love, and enjoy each other very easily, and that is the goal from ancient times as well as today that cultures aim towards. The great people of humanity are the simplest persons, but they have a vast human love. They have hearts of great humanity, and they live in humanity, in gratitude and in repayment, and become great people, who both individuals and society have recognized.

The duty of a child to care for parents in a thoughtful manner is indispensable. The Buddhist point of view also recognizes your important responsibility to parents who have not known the Buddhist teachings. The child should introduce the Dharma to parents, so that they can study, practice the relief of suffering. The Buddha said: "Those who repay their parents for their nourishment by donating material goods will never give enough to repay their parents. But my children, whose parents do not have faith in the Three Jewels, please encourage your parents to believe in the Three Jewels, to parents who live in an ungodly way, give them the encouragement to be holy. For the parents who have become greedy, try to encourage them to do charity work. For the parents of wrong view, encourage them to turn to the right view. Then you will fulfill your complete thanks to your mother and father."

The above teachings show you that filial piety has the same path as the liberation of the Dharma that is the life of cultivating consciousness. The teachings of the Buddha open a new direction for life. Everyone acknowledges that all people aspire to peace and liberation. However, the nature of life is always changing and impermanent; it is very difficult for people to have true happiness if they only live with material measurements. Although you have a lot of material to serve your parents, these things can only be fulfilled physically, for the true happiness of man is not only material but spiritual and those teachings have the power to transform and heal suffering. Learning and practicing the dharma is going on the path of wisdom in a way that helps parents come away from all the greed of suffering.

Wisdom can bring you to a calm life and awareness, to help you see the root of suffering, from which the idea of self, the evil mind is removed. Only the practice of Dharma gives your parents a true way of life, resting firmly, step by step moving away from the cycle of suffering into happiness, to live peacefully in the present life. The way of happiness that your parents are choosing, is really the long way, the real road, so it is your most filial way.

189
HAPPINESS IS GRATEFULNESS

The gift that you give to your parents by living a calm, peaceful and relaxed life, and introducing that blissful happiness to them is the most precious gift you ever offer to both of the people who gave birth to you. Because this gift is very long lasting, it creates happiness from a pure soul, with no selfishness, greed, or ego, and it leads to an altruistic life, mindful and benevolent. In this way, you will discover that happiness is the noblest goal in life, morality and humanity, and this is the road that leads to happiness for you and the others; with each step and in each breath, gratitude and humanity are the seeds of true happiness in life.

Happiness is synonymous with a life of selflessness, compassion, and selflessness, and thus responsibility for self-happiness becomes a duty of responsibility for others' well-being, plus the benefit of society. The greater the level of practicing compassion and selflessness, the happier and more lasting the happiness will be. When the heart opens, suffering will close, altruism will open to everyone, then your happiness will be the happiness of everyone; in other words, another's happiness is your happiness.

The concept of gratitude and human life will lead to a harmonious attitude of people towards family, society, and their country as a duty to self and happiness. It is a spiritual dimension, a conscious way of life that modern society needs to pay attention. The selflessness and compassion of Buddhism have given life to mankind to bring forth the human love which flows into a precious and beautiful life.

Here we can conclude that the pinnacle of life is to live with human love and the Buddha's teachings have the same view of the heart opening as gratitude and repayment. These two entities have been going and will continue to flow into the hearts of humanity to soothe the painful and hateful wounds of human life. In the contemporary society of eternal civilization and intimate friendship, it is desirable to build a non-violent, worldly, peaceful community. Each of us needs to establish the foundation of compassion, selflessness, and not-self that begins with the virtue of filial piety, the human life of gratitude and repayment. It likes this that happiness is spread from family to community, from the nation to the whole world.

The Buddha indicates the root of all troubles, suffering, is based on attachment, anger, and lack of discernment, and when the evil mind arises, the heart of selfishness, conflict, and confrontation exist. The path to happiness is the path of altruism and compassion. In this way, you are fully responsible for yourself in this life, not to be interfered with by any invisible sinner. That teaching is a true human way of life, human beings are the root, and you can determine your life and destiny which are based on experimental value that human love is the beginning of the values of happiness and the process of liberation. Buddhism does not go into a world of imagination; the Buddha has shown you that in you there are the virtues of mindfulness, compassion, tolerance, and wisdom that are natural. Psychologists have found and shown us that humans have a tremendous amount of intelligence in their brains, but only with very little intelligence is human love forgotten and replaced by feelings of lust.

Let yourself live to the depths to know that there are wonderful things around you, and to show your gratitude to the earth, the flowers, the grass, the hills that have been given to you as part of a wonderful life, and especially for the two who gave birth to you. Let your soul be watered again with a loving heart and great humanity, so that all on this earth may sing in the stream of love and compassion.

> *"Whoever in this life*
> *Knows how to be grateful to parents*
> *Remember the grace of all species*
> *Happiness is gratefulness."*

28

STUDYING BUDDHA'S TEACHING

"The Buddha's teaching means that it has the power to transform suffering, to suppress defilements, and to achieve joy during practice."

The rapid development of scientific and technological advances has led to a large number of people living in crowded urban centers. Instead of interacting with nature, with people around to talk to, helping each other when needed, people today are so dependent on machinery for human beings' services. In the past when you needed food, you would have to walk miles to buy it, but now you just use the phone, and in a moment, you will have people bring food to your door. Everybody wants to have their own homes, cars, telephones, etc... and tend to be independent without relying on one another, and enjoy the results of scientific achievements. The reverse side of that development is an awareness that you can be self-reliant without depending on those around you. That makes the future of humanity something to worry about, because other people are not important in your life, so the happiness or suffering of another person has nothing to do with you. Sometimes street robberies are still ignored by passersby.

Modern society has created an environment where people live in isolation and are becoming lonely and lost as they become addicted to their devices. Although humans live side by side, their interactions with each other have slowly begun to fade into the background as they become consumed by technology. Instead of living in the now, providing support for each other, contributing to each other, everyone only exists in an insensible role, now acting instead as an automated machine that breathes and moves. Very few people are aware of this problem because everyone has ambivalent competition and ambition for material needs. The prevailing psychological and emotional suffering has invaded Western society and developed nations. This has been caused by the market-oriented lifestyle and the lack of contemporary spiritual life. People have a reason to follow the success of scientific technology because of the fascination that it has brought: instant gratification. The practice of the spiritual training of the mind is only the result of the invisible part for which people now have limited patience.

Fortunately, in such advanced society there are some who have realized this problem. They have known that true happiness is a grip on the welfare of modern science, the power of knowledge to do business for the material life. At the same time, they learn about the spiritual life to nourish the spirit. A person of profound insights into geographical astronomy, being extremely wealthy but lacking spiritual life will never reach true happiness. Sometimes the prosperity of material goods lacking of morality is a dangerous disaster. This is very important, so you should be aware of it and not rely too much on scientific achievement. Many have believed in science and negated the importance of spirituality, claiming that there is no evidence of the power of spiritual value and that morality is only based on personal preferences. Meanwhile, scientists and philosophers who seek to find an absolute truth or immutable law have a very solid spiritual life. This shows a complete reversal of humanity in society now and mainstream science.

There is no intention to criticize the dedication of science, especially how technology has enabled us to make miraculous discoveries, such as landing on the moon, and discovering alien galaxies. The concern here is how we apply science to life to match reality and balance body and mind. It is a challenge for human beings in current society to find out how they can both enjoy scientific achievements and bring both the spiritual life and the balance between body and mind in the midst of the dawn and the new millennium.

It is not obvious that the Buddha advised you not to give up the opportunity to learn and practice his teachings. From Pali, *Dhammassavanaṃ* means the hearing of preaching of the teaching of the Buddha. His teaching has the power to transform suffering, to suppress defilements, and to achieve joy during practice. Every man needs religious beliefs to feed his life. We rely on religion so that there is no helplessness in the realm of illusions, to understand that it is precious and that it is worthy. However, you need to understand the difference between religious belief and spiritual life. Religion involves faith through offering prayer to a savior of a religious tradition. When you feel small before a vast universe, all things find you lost in the middle of the world of illusion, and you accept a supernatural power, then offer yourself to a doctrine or Supreme Being to be comforted by prayer through blessing. Meanwhile, spirituality is the practice to arouse the virtuous qualities of human beings such as love, compassion, forgiveness, tolerance, affection, patience, harmony, and responsibility. Water the good seeds to make you fresher, happier, and more peaceful. Happiness comes when you realize the cause of suffering, transforming the mind from hatred and anger to forgiveness. When you are suffering, you can stand beneath a supreme being to recite, to cry or to perform any ritual to pray for an invisible miracle to give you strength to overcome these difficulties. It is also essential in human life to serve the masses, a fascinating seduction just like opium mesmerizes human beings. However, turning to religion by only participating in the power of prayer and abandoning the self-effort to practice promoting the virtues of the heart is a great omission.

Thus, everyone can develop that virtue through constant learning and training of the mind. Each person has a good seed, and one can water the seed not only by practicing and following the Buddhist tradition, but also by practicing other religions. I believe that the spiritual leaders of all religious traditions on this planet are honoring and encouraging people to seek the truth, happiness and beauty in life.

> "Do not miss the chance to study the Buddha's teaching
> Diligence tirelessly
> the mind will relax with light heartedness
> Then live a peaceful life."

29

PRACTICING PATIENCE

"In our lives, sometimes we have to deal with problems caused by jealousy and selfishness. However, we should not be discouraged. The more challenges we face, the better the chances for us to learn and be more mature. Challenges are like nutrition for our spiritual lives."

Consider this story about teaching patience: There was a novice living in the practice meditation center with his master, who was a Zen master. It was fall season. Every morning, the novice had to sweep the fallen leaves to clean the temple's patio and welcome guests. One morning, he awoke to a quiet place and no sign of visitors. There was nothing except a pile of leaves on the ground. He quickly cleaned up the leaves and put them in the trash. He then looked up into the tree. There were still a lot of leaves which were turning color and ready to fall. He thought if he shook off the leaves from the tree and cleaned them up then, he would save himself the work tomorrow. He looked for a way to climb up the tree. After the novice made a few steps up the tree, his master suddenly appeared near the tree and looked up at him. The master said: "Dear son, be patient and wait until the leaves fall off!" The novice immediately climbed down and greeted his master. He felt ashamed for his clumsy thought. The master smiled, forgave him, and walked into the Buddha hall. The novice realized that his action showed immaturity and impatience. Not only had the master just saved the tree and saved the novice from falling off the tree, but he also taught the student to be patient.

In Pali, *Khantī* means patience, forbearance, forgiveness. Patience can be practiced in many different ways: enduring the suffering brought by others; staying calm when facing slander, libel, or unwanted things; forgiving someone even when he hurts or insults you; patiently doing good deeds for others; accepting blame or praise in life. True love always has practiced patience. Patience is the source of happiness.

In general, people tend to be less happy when others are more beautiful, more successful, smarter, or even faster in practicing Buddhism. We tend to be poor in praising those who are successful because we are afraid of diminishing our own value in doing so. If someone gives compliments to someone else, we tend to interrupt and add: "yes, he is good, but …". We tend to be jealous of a person who has better qualities than we do.

PRACTICING PATIENCE

There has never been great responsibility given to an inexperienced person who lacks willpower and patience. If we look closely, we realize that those who have experienced much bitterness in their lives have the energy and patience to carry on great work in life. Some examples are great people of humanity like Mahatma Gandhi and Nelson Mandela. Mandela had experienced many in life to bring justice for the people of South Africa. Gandhi focused his life on peace, happiness, and prosperity for the Indian people against British exploitation. Such examples show that in order to make great fame, we need extraordinary patience. Sometimes, success does not come after just one, two, or three tries, but may take many tries. In order to achieve these accomplishments, we must begin by practicing patience.

A person who practices patience has a natural glowing appearance. He does not need sparkling suits, but he himself illuminates the surounding space. I remember a colorful conversation between my master and a popular professor from a well-known university. The professor asked: "What are the differences between Buddhism and Christianity? Between the Buddha and the Christian God? Between the Buddha's teachings and Christian Bible? What is Buddha Dhamma? Where does Buddhist meditation come from? ..." My master was benign and merciful. He smiled and then slowly answered the questions without controversy. He said: "A beautiful corolla must have a combination of many different kinds of flowers. It is not the case that a chrysanthemum is less beautiful than a rose, or an apricot blossom is prettier than a dahlia. Each flower has its own characteristics. The same concept applies to religions. Each belief has its own sacred qualities, which enriches the activities and practices of humanity. Many religious beliefs differ in their philosophical ideas but they have the capacity to co-exist and complement each other."

One can believe in the religion he is practicing, taking refuge in a spiritual teacher. However, he should not contemplate the philosophy of religions. Making comparisons between religions, e.g., which is strong, which is weak, which is high, which is low, is the source of contradictions. Some people believe in the Buddha and practice Buddha's teachings. Others believe in God and practice God's words from the Bible. There is no need to prove this practice is better than others. We should be kind to others, beautify our lives, and make individuals like flowers in the garden of mankind.

Jealousy is a very common problem that we all have to face. Not only lay people but also monastics who dedicate their lives to practicing selflessness have to deal with resentment. If someone is more successful than others, naturally this creates envy. In order to stay successful, he must maintain his patience and persevere with his work to the end result. For example, the Dalai Lama, is the emissary of peace for the human being, who has great influence on many people, was often confronted by the Shugden community every time he traveled and preached in the United State and Europe. Despite protests and noise from the Shugden, the Dalai Lama has worked hard to deliver peaceful messages and bring love to mankind. He is a great example of one who practices patience.

Following in the footsteps of the Dalai Lama, we should never be discouraged when facing the difficulties of jealousy. Instead, we should consider these difficulties as opportunities for us to practice patience and maturity in our spiritual lives. The more difficulties, the better the chances for us to achieve patience. Humiliation, slander, and libel are fuel for habitude of patience and virtue of tolerance. These are necessary qualities to brace us against unknown future problems so that we can accomplish the larger goals of our lives. In addition, consider obstacles as opportunities that give us positive ways of thinking and solving problems. In short, practicing patience is the key to success.

Sometimes, not only does our patience deal with problems from the external environment, but from our own physical bodies as well. When our bodies become ill, we may feel sad, helpless, or hopeless because our daily activities seem to be suspended. In addition, when sick we tend to want everybody's attention. If no one is around, we feel lonely and bored. In other words, when the body is not healthy, the mind is impaired and this could lead to an imbalanced life. We also need to be patient with strong and healthy bodies, especially as youths. Young people are full of energy, but they can get lost in a society of temptations. In order to guide their powerful bodies to do the right things, we must put them in good environments, find their talents and train them in the right skills.

When dealing with our bodies, either ill or healthy, young or old, we must be patient. Our patience helps us to understand the capabilities of the body in every situation. Once we have knowledge about our own bodies, we either accept them or patiently train them to achieve our goals in life. We ultimately obtain the highest satisfaction when our bodies and our minds work together.

Incrementally, dealing with our minds requires greater patience. Naturally, the mind is unstable. It never stops thinking nonsense. It's comparing what we have and what we don't and thinking things like "The grass on the other side is always greener!"

In order to prevent the wandering mind, we must often observe and guide it to positive thinking. With patience of the mind, we can reduce the bad influences on our daily decisions. There are many examples in life and history that show the great results of people learning to control their minds. The following conversation between Buddha and his disciple, Punna,[60] is an example of a great mind:

"Dear Punna, the people of Sunaparanta are rough, if they scold and abuse you, what will you do?

PRACTICING PATIENCE

Lord Buddha, if the people of Sunaparanta scold and abuse me, it will occur to me, indeed the people of Sunaparanta are good, they do not hurt me with their hands.

Dear Punna, if the people of Sunaparanta hurt you with their hands, what will you do?

Lord Buddha, if the people of Sunaparanta hurt me with their hands, it will occur to me, indeed the people of Sunaparanta are good, they do not hurt me with clods.

Dear Punna, if the people of Sunaparanta hurt you with clods, what will you do?

Lord Buddha, if the people of Sunaparanta hurt me with clods, it will occur to me, indeed the people of Sunaparanta are good, they do not hurt me with a stick.

Dear Punna, if the people of Sunaparanta hurt you with a stick, what will you do?

Lord Buddha, if the people of Sunaparanta hurt me with a stick, it will occur to me, indeed the people of Sunaparanta are good, they do not hurt me with a weapon

Dear Punna, if the people of Sunaparanta hurt you with a weapon, what will you do?

Lord Buddha, if the people of Sunaparanta hurt me with a weapon, it will occur to me, indeed the people of Sunaparanta are good, they do not end my life with a sharp weapon.

Dear Punna, if the people of Sunaparanta put an end to your life with a sharp weapon, what will you do?

Lord Buddha, if the people of Sunaparanta would put an end to my life, it will occur to me thus. There are disciples of the Blessed One, who loathing the body and life search for an assassin. Here I have got an assassin even without a search.

Good! Punna, it is possible for you to abide in Sunaparanta endowed with that appeasement in the Teaching. You may do the fit now."

Buddha expressed happiness for Punna. He said Punna had achieved a state in which nothing could disturb him, even the threat of death. Additionally, he held no ill will toward those who would harm him. Patience, compassion, and happiness are recipes for peace and leisure. Punna was patient when facing insults, threats, scolding, beating, and killing. Being in difficult situations is actually a good condition in which people may practice patience. Conversely, if we all lived in a nice environment where there was no conflict, where no one made others angry, then we would not need patience. In other words, we simply hold off our emotions when facing problems to avoid calamity, hatred, or sorrow. Punna is a great example for us to learn by and practice patience.

How do we start practicing patience? Let's start with an easy exercise by counting steps. Every morning, let's count the number of steps we walk to work. We may miss count the first time, but make sure we succeed the next one. In addition, we can practice sitting calmly and counting our breaths with mindfulness: "Breath in and I know I am breathing in, breath out and I know I am breathing out." We count from one to ten and then repeat the cycle. If the count does not yet reach ten, but our mind is already distracted, we have to start back at one. These exercises help us to gain patience not only through the body but also through the mind. Let's start with easy exercises and step by step we will try more difficult ones.

Learning and practicing how to nurture patience is a must. Wherever we go or whatever we do, we need a strong will and a strong mind. If our patience is nurtured every day, our compassion will be greater and we will see people with love and respect. We may face difficult circumstances in life or meet someone who is not very easy to deal with, but we can smile and accept him because we know that he also has his own suffering. It is important that our patience is present at all times so that we always gain happiness in the here and now.

> *"Practicing patience*
> *The mind is firmly grounded*
> *Smiling with waves of life*
> *Leads to happiness and satisfaction."*

30

THE SHAME OF MISTAKES

"Controlling our emotions not only sharpens our judgement but also makes others around us more comfortable because of our honesty"

Once a person has a closed mind, he won't be able to learn good ideas from others. There will be less opportunities to receive advice to correct his mistakes. Being ashamed enables one to open his mind to solutions from others.

Sovacassatā in Pali means shame. It also means a virtuous person, who is able to listen and accept good advice from others. Listening and changing to right from wrong is not easy if we don't have mindfulness. Many of us think: "I was born this way. I don't want to change myself into an unnatural personality" or "I did not do anything wrong. People who can bear me stay!" These behaviors most likely come from selfishness, where one makes mistakes but does not want to listen to others' criticisms. He chooses to be alone rather than being with those who want him to change. This stubbornness and lack of conscience is a way to protect the self of a self-centered person.

Shame is vital. In its absence, suffering continues and may accumulate. For example, consider an employee who is frequently late to work, misses deadlines, and lacks self-motivation. He denies his responsibility when confronted with these problems. For a while, he feels that his boss and colleagues hate him, and then he quits. Not only this employee, but anyone who can't see his mistake is miserable. The more he tries to flee from problems that he creates, and the more he excuses his behavior, the more he suffers.

Let's examine further the aforementioned employee. He was a victim of his own self: emotionally dominant and not guided by conscience. His shameless behavior prevented harmony at work and cost him his job. He ended up a failed person in society. Why would someone have such an attitude? What would he have lost if he had sat down, listened to others about his behavior, and changed himself into a better person and a better employee? Being aware of the self, realizing its weaknesses, and overcoming the inferiority complex are necessary elements for a successful life.

On the other hand, we should all remember that a person like that employee, who doesn't have the ability to accept his own faults because of his self-centeredness, is very miserable. We should not use his mistakes to attack him. A heavy sword cannot cut soft silk. Instead, we should give him more care and love to help him overcome the situation. We need tolerance to overcome the awkward. Loving speech and a gentle attitude are just enough to transform this self-centered person.

I know many people who struggle and cannot listen to criticism from others, for the better. They always find reasons to defend their ego. When they hurt someone, instead of saying sorry, they try hard to find reasons to prove they did nothing wrong. They cover their faults and hope to gain respect from others. Instead, they often get the opposite results. People look at them as fools who lack understanding of social morals. On the other hand, I also know many people who have a subtle attitude of accepting mistakes and listening to learn. They gain respect from others and most importantly they get benefits from learning from their mistakes. If the employee from our story were listening to others, understanding his weaknesses and changing his behaviors, he would be happy in his job and have a lot of friends and a happy family.

Another common behavior occurs when one wants to cover his faults, gets angry easily, or makes the asumption that everybody is against him. He shows abnormal behaviors and makes others uncomfortable. As a result, he is untrusted and rejected by others. In other words, without acknowledging the shame of our own mistakes people can easily get into these conditions in life.

People whose actions depend on emotions without reasoning for the consequences experience suffering, because emotion is not independent. Emotion changes over time, like the weather in Seattle: shining sun in the morning and rain in the afternoon. Sigmund Freud, the great psychologist, said that people can control a part of the brain which can control the self; clumsiness is the blind part of the brain. The Buddha even showed us how to focus on our own breath so that we can achieve mindfulness to control our thought, action, and speech. Mindfulness is the key to overcoming all emotions and being aware of our mistakes: "Breathing in, I see the damages I caused to myself; breathing out, I am aware of the suffering I cause to myself." Once we recognize the causes of problems, we then practice: "Breathing in, I sincerely change myself for the better and determine to restart with a clean slate; breathing out, I vow not to repeat the mistake."

A person who can filter emotions from thought and course of actions can not only sharpen his own judgement but also gain support from others around him because of his humble characteristics. Stubbornness and refusal to admit our errors do not gain us anything, but instead alienates others. In order to be successful in our personal and business relationships, we must prepare ourselves with the ability to accept our mistakes. A gentle, cheerful attitude and acceptance of our own faults results in more than fifty percent of our success. Knowing these rules is like knowing human beings, nature, and the universe. The more we know, the better our chances of doing the right things throughout life.

Furthermore, if one tries to improve his personality by accepting mistakes, he must be honest and start with sincerity from the heart. We should improve ourselves by looking to virtuous, responsible examples of human civilization and carrying out a higher purpose. If one is a farmer, he must work hard to produce not only quantity, but quality of flowers, vegetables, and fruits. A professor must work hard to enrich his knowledge and transfer it to his students. Legislators are constantly rethinking laws to improve people's lives. Psychologists constantly learn to provide good practice for patients. Inventors are constantly inventing new smart phones, computers, cars, camcorders, sound recorders and more. In general, people need nutrition and exercise to enhance the body. They also need peace and happiness for the mind. All three aspects of human life (the physical, mental, and emotional) must be properly nurtured to build our perfect day every day.

A young or old person has the ability to recognize his own faults and make corrections. Psychologists have proved that even the elderly who have strong will can learn new professions easily. Success depends not on age but on will and determination. Older people gain their habits due to repetitive actions in life. Even a child has habits of consciousness from previous lives. In order to convert bad habits, we must see the benefits of listening, accepting and changing to be better. We will be more relaxed, less stressed, and happier. We will gain more opportunities to succeed in life. Refusing counsel, closing the heart, and not accepting wrongdoing is a sign of suffering and unhappiness. Most of the arts require painstaking study. However, the art of recognizing one's own mistakes does not require much effort. We just need to listen and accept our faults to change for our own happiness and for the happiness of others.

> *"Whoever lives in this life*
> *Who is ashamed of his own mistakes*
> *Greed is out from him*
> *Happiness will follow."*

31

JOINING WITH SPIRITUAL LIFE

> *"By the Sangha, you have the opportunity to learn and practice the teachings of the Buddha. The role of Buddhism in ethics is first and foremost the orientation of normative life, the education of living beings, which is essential in today's society where ethics show signs of being forgotten."*

Everybody can learn and practice Dharma anywhere at anytime. While the "honest work for honest pay" principle applies, the Buddha still emphasized that practice without direction by monks can be ineffective due to the preoccupation and stress caused by work and family. Children and spousal demands tend to be especially inexhaustible. Given such tremendous distractions, our plan for practicing at home might not be accomplished.

Realizing these challenges, the Buddha suggested learning his teachings from *samana*, or monks. These monastics devote their lives to studying Dharma, bringing the teachings to society. Because of their dedication to and expertise in Buddhism, monks can be good teachers for any layperson who wishes to learn effectively.

Connecting with monks, one is directed to find Buddhist treasure: the wisdom of kindness. Compassion, forgiveness and control of the ego are core teachings that monks are obligated to introduce to society. While these values are often forgotten in modern times, they are essential for promoting love and happiness and for reducing suffering.

Through the images of a simple life led by monks and disciples of the Buddha, we learn to share pain and suffering with others. These images directly and indirectly affect morale in society. They advise people to do good deeds and be generous to others who lack merits. Thus, practicing the Buddha's teachings is to bring peace to society and prevents revenge, hate, and discrimination. Buddhist morality intends to improve life in contemporary society. His teachings enlighten and lead mankind to overcome unpleasant things in life and to share love, peace and happiness. Buddha's teaching contains powerful strength that helps people face daily challenges. Where virtue exists, there is happiness; where wisdom exists, there is peace. Wisdom is like our eyes and virtue is our feet. Virtue is like a car that takes us wherever we want to go and wisdom is like the key that opens the door for us. Thus, happiness or suffering is the way of life of each person. No one can bless or dislodge anyone. If we live a virtuous and honest life, happiness will be present. Heaven always opens its welcoming doors to all of us, not just to the devoted or to religious/ sectarian monopolies.

Buddha's teachings are logical and proven by science, which clears doubt and helps people improve their way of life. When one comes to study with Buddhist masters, they will learn that this religion does not divide people into two groups: believers who reach salvation and non-believers who are abandoned. Instead, they will be encouraged by the teachings to exert themselves with the power of liberation, to let go of the old bad habits to become lovable, good people in life. They learn not to believe in a supernatural being other than themselves. Believing in the effectiveness and power of meditation can lead people to self-conquest; to be aware of what is happening around them; and to control emotions, which will reduce daily stresses.

> "Close to the monastics
> Have oppontunity to study hard Buddha's teachings
> Illuminate the world
> Like the full moonlight."

32

ATTENDING DHARMA SHARING

"Attending dharma sharing helps us to exchange knowledge and experience with others. This is a good way to learn about other cultures and open our minds to the world."

One beautiful morning weekend, two friends meet and greet. What do they talk about? One talks about a movie she watched last week, a neighborhood story, a trip to New York, a city with skyscrapers, etc. The other friend tries to listen and wait for an opportunity to add her opinions.

Such conversations are very common. People tend to embellish their own self value. What is the benefit of self-aggrandizement? Bragging does not gain any respect from others. It may temporarily satisfy one's self interest, but it has no meaning to others. My friend has confessed that over the last thirty years, he had not been paying attention when I talked about playing football and watching the World Cup, Champions League, Premier League, La Liga, etc.

Dhammasakkaccha in Pali means meaningful talk. The Buddha advised us to make sure our conversations are beneficial and interesting to others. The attitude of the speaker and the listener must be open, attentive and happy. The art of communicating is to draw the attention of the audience. We must speak well and discuss interesting topics. Everybody is happy when talking to a person who is cheerful and engaging; especially someone who exhibits a strong personality, openness, problem-solving and decision-making skills.

Someone who listens to others in a conversation can easily gain good relationships at work or anywhere he goes. When listening attentively with compassion, we make people feel good. Even when we have an urgent issue, we must be calm and make sure the listener is ready to listen. This way we can deliver the message efficiently. Very few people understand that an effective conversation requires not only the speaker but the listener as well. They must effectively exchange ideas in the conversation.

The most important factors in an effective conversation are the participation of all parties and the general morale of the event. All concerns of participants are discussed and proper resolutions are reached in a timely manner. A clever speaker must consider and properly address the audience's concerns. In order to understand the audience's problems, he should often interrupt his speech, listen and answer questions before continuing with his points. Especially in one-on-one conversations, it is very annoying if one just talks without giving others the chance to participate.

Although animals can't speak, they do make sound and have ways to communicate with the world around them. Fish in a pond are splashing water by waving their tails in the water to draw visitors' attention and to ask for food. As one drops a piece of bread into the pond, they immediately jump for the food and wave their tails to the air, as if to thank him. A dog greets his owner when he gets home by jumping to him, licking his face, barking happily, and wagging his tail to draw the owner's attention and to show his love to the owner.

Humans, the most intelligent mammels, have the capability to communicate using oral, written, or sign language. Sign language can express fun or anger, calmness or urgency, smiling or frowning, humming or screaming, etc. Language or sign language affects others directly or indirectly. Depending on the mood of your emotions, others want to be with you, and they tend to agree with you or not. Thus, it is important to learn to live in harmony and have effective communications with others.

Sociologists agree that the primary purpose of education is to train people to be persuasive and well-spoken. Mutual conversation is very important in modern society particularly. People need instant information to react properly to the changes of the world. They also need to extend their friendships to the world. An interesting conversation carries important information; i.e.: a good idea or a new event, which can be applied in everyday life. Bringing a clear message, or presenting facts or ideas, that benefit others is vital for effective communication. In Buddhist tradition, there are conversational meetings without talking, where people attending the meeting just sit quietly. Each individual is aware of the presence of each other with joy, peacefulness, and happiness.

Society and individuals are always governed by language. Whether conversation brings peace or war, depends on the language. Psychologists treat patients using language. Words have such extraordinary power to change the world. However, there must be sincerity and compassion. For example, when one is angry and screaming, he makes others miserable. Instead, with tolerance and understanding, he just needs to speak softly to persuade others. In addition, we must do what we say and say what we do to gain trust from others. When others believe in us, they believe in what we say.

Language is the means by which humans exchange thoughts and ideas. Written language describes thoughts progressively. Language helps people to come closer to each other through dialogue. Through language, human beings can discover the conquest of the beautiful universe and the mysterious world around them. Humans are the most civilized among animals because of their language and their use of dialogue.

Participating in conversations means to share and exchange experiences and learn from each other. Through conversations, we understand more about culture and people. We gain knowledge so that we can move forward on the path of life. A successful person is one who constantly learns, actively participates in conversations, and uses language cleverly to express his thoughts. Last but not least, those who find the virtues of others are loved and admired.

> *"Attending the dharma sharing*
> *Learning good things,*
> *Glowing in this life*
> *Gaining respect from others."*

33

LIFE IS A MIRACLE

"Sometimes the other person is blinded by the veil of ignorance, trapped by wrong idea; therefore, do not give him the purpose of life, the meaning of his life. With detachment from the wrong perception then he can relate to the beautiful, the good and find the direction in life.

India is one of the most religious countries worldwide. Brahmanism was later changed to Hinduism as the oldest surviving Hindu cult of the Ganga river and Bārānasī at the north. According to Brāhmaṇa, in the world created by Brahma, he who wants to change his destiny must have the method and the supplication of the supreme leaders in Brahman, and they believe in praying to the Brahma. That lifestyle is thought to have gone deeply into the India or Indian culture.

From the Pali, we have the word *Tapa*, which is torment, punishment, penance, self-ascetic practice. Tapa is used by the Hindu masters to describe the process of human beings when they first came out, grew up, married, followed a peaceful life, then studied religion. Tapa practice is sitting under the sky and then burning fire around you; initially the fire is further away from the practitioner, but when practicing for a long time one sits closer to the fire. Meditators study meditation to a degree that it no longer feels hot. Such practice in Hindu is called burning affliction.

Sometimes the Buddha also uses foreign words to explain the teachings for modern people to understand more easily but have the specific meaning of Buddhist teachings. For example, Dana means donation. Hindu teachers teach believers to kill animals to offer to Brahma, while the Buddha uses the word Dana as a gift of joy for life, a joy that can be a loaf of bread for a homeless person, an old coat for the unfortunate, or helping a person to lessen their fear. All these things must be done with a delighted heart that does not expect anything in return. The word Brahma, in Hinduism, is understood as the lord who created the universe and all beings, including humans and sentient beings. In Buddhism, Brahma is understood as the parents. The other meaning of the Brahma word in Hinduism is the person who has a deep understanding of Vedas scripture. In Buddhism Brahma indicates the person who eliminates afflictions.

From Pali, *Tapa* in Buddhist practice means effort, the patience to learn about life, to live deeply and meaningfully.

Imagine warming up, warming up enthusiasm in your heart, because afflictions often disturb your mind, not letting the mind be calm, so you have to burn them. *Tapa* has another meaning: that it is more important to use wisdom to observe the mind to know who you are and what you are doing with your life. Do you really live a meaningful life?

Many of us have spent a whole day trying to work on a project, a construction, reaching a status, or accomplishing a dream that was cherished. We do not just use our labor strength, but also use our intelligence to pursue these goals which interferes in the care of organizing a daily life worth living. We think about the future and are not able to live in the present. The human condition of consciousness is very limited because people are limited by their sadness, anxiety, anger, fear and hiding. To be more precise, people do not enjoy life completely, but live as a dreamer rather than a living consciousness. Meditation will help you awaken from a deep sleep with unconscious machinery actions.

Be aware of the emotions and healing the unwholesome mind in order to nurture happiness in all. Thousands of years ago the Buddha discovered that the miracle of life is realized only when you are aware of what you have. Through that process, the teachings of the Buddha have brought great benefits to today's society, especially those living in a busy society, as it can help them balance the culture that always wants to possess, wants to own nature, rather than being aware that man is a very intimate part of human life. When you know how to look deeply inside with a clear, systematic method, you have the ability to live a more harmonious, happy, meaningful, and peaceful life. Just being aware and paying attention will give you a new perspective on the world around you, which can complement the narrow materialistic ideas that govern thought and invade human culture.

The more you chase material goods, the more tired you are, and the empty mood forces you to find something to fill the void. Often you avoid feeling melancholy with alcohol, drugs, going to the bar, all to fill the emptiness and loneliness in your heart. Psychologists say that a decade ago, university students in Europe lived about 60 percent with a purpose in life, while college students in the United States were less than 30 percent. The existential vacuum is a disease in current times, not only a symptom of individuals but also collective society. Not feeling life, feeling depressed, not finding illumination, then looking for means, joy to forget, which guides people to the path of suffering and violence.

We need to find a way to help young people get a living energy, find the meaning of life, know what to live for, who to live for, to live for righteousness. No one can give a meaning to standard life, this is the mainstream, ~~you~~ use it! The task of the spiritual teacher is to find the Buddha's teachings, provide you with a method to illuminate ignorance, help you find the true meaning of life, understand it.

Sometimes people say, this life is so boring, there is no meaning to life. People are covered by pain from year to year. When facing such cases, what can we do to help them? It is difficult to give advice or an idea, a formula or doctrine for them to practice. The first thing to do is to understand and look deeply to understand, recognize the gifted, good things of the person, and provide them with a method for growing the good seeds in them. The Buddha taught, everyone has good seed, which is called Bodhichitta. When the Bodhi seed is manifested, they get their vitality back. It would be very difficult to know how to water a good seed without knowing anything about the past and the way in which they live today. The fire in the heart has been hurt not only by words but by an ideal meaningful life, compassionate heart, loving kindness, and purity of purpose all help the heart. When you have the goal of living and shedding joy, that energy spreads and the person has the opportunity to come back to discover in themselves something beautiful that has long been blocked and suppressed. Sometimes the other person is blinded by the veil, trapped in a wrong idea, so he does not have purpose or meaning in his life. With detachment of the wrong perception, he can contact the beautiful, the good, and find direction in life.

In life you need a deep desire, which is called the food of volition. Thanks to that dream, you have the energy to overcome the difficulties in life. Those who are depressed, who have no purpose in life, cannot find the joy and true meaning of life. Nelson Mandela is a hero of the South African nation. Before he became president, he was in prison for 27 years. In the bad conditions of detention, it is very easy for victims to despair. But Mandela found a way to live. He witnessed many people being executed, many of whom read the bible before dying to prove that they had faith in God and regarded death as normal. The death of a prisoner with faith and their calmness made him calm. So, he was determined to nurture the idea and the beautiful desire to resist the suffering, sickness, and hunger in prison.

You can only find the meaning of life when you want to do something in life. For example, you may want to pursue a college degree, a career of your choice, a beautiful ideal. When you discover a talent for music, writing music is not necessarily for fame, for profit, or for copyright, but for your good intentions. Your career is to live and show your talent that makes life more beautiful, to contribute to the arts. Or if you have the talent of an artist as well, your work can bring joy and fun for viewers. The picture carries a message that helps many people forget the sorrows of life.

Siddhartha wanted to find a way to transform suffering and help mankind to escape it, but power like that of his father, king Suddhodana, could not help. This thought helped Siddhartha overcome the difficulties of the ascetic practice: the sky is as a blanket, the land as pillows surrounded by mountains and forests in winter, hot sun dried his skin in summer. For six years wandering to find a way of liberation, Siddhartha came to consult with many schools, many masters, including the ascetic practice to make the body dry and skinny, and exhausted, he almost died.

Thanks to the thought of wanting to save people's life, Siddhartha overcame all difficulties and survived. The desire to give the joy of his life never ceased, but became even stronger after Siddhartha's enlightenment. He spent 45 years teaching to the masses how he had become enlightened and trained many of his monastics in his sangha. The truth is, Buddha does not want to receive respect and honor and also does not want to be famous. Siddhartha's message is only to show man the cause of suffering and transform suffering into happiness, bringing happiness to life. Thus, the true meaning of life is that there is something real to be done in order to live on.

In addition to pursuing a beautiful dream or a noble ideal, love adds meaning to life. Love can be love for Buddha, God, or love for men or women. Everyone wants to love and looks forward to love; that is the natural necessity of human beings. When there is love, you have vitality, and you start discovering the new thing or the beauty in yourself and the one you love. Trinh Cong Son said: "Living in this life is only the body and love. The body is finite, love is infinite, how we can nourish love so that love can redeem the body on the cross of life." According to him, love is the only way to save the human species, without love we cannot survive. However, I think when we love others, to understand the person we love, we must understand ourselves first. We cannot understand who we are! What do we want in life? We cannot love others for long. True love is the journey to seek, explore yourself as long as you discover the person you love. If you do not understand who you are, you cannot understand the person you love. Buddha is one who is endowed with right understanding in the world because he knows himself. Where there is deep understanding, there is greater love. Understanding will give us the ability to love the other, help the other have less suffering.

In the Third of the five mindfulness trainings, an important message is "I vow to not have sexual relationship to anyone without morally true love and long-lasting commitments." The true relationship between man and woman is something holy; otherwise it is a devastating action. True love can give you more energy to live forward and have more vitality. When we are in love, we can sacrifice energy and sacrifice our life for the loved one. The essential element is to understand the person you love. The ability to understand depends on the ability to practice, deep practice is to know and love ourselves first and then we will have the ability to understand and love others. If we do not understand, then we suffer. In the Buddhist spirit, love is a discovery. If we cannot liberate ourselves, how do we liberate others? When we have not found the meaning of our lives, how can we help others find the meaning of their lives?

To look and observe the plants, the grass, we will see that plants and grass still need love and care. Look at the large leaves and the smaller leaves of the coconut palm. The older leaves absorb the light, absorb carbon dioxide, transfer nutrients to grow the younger coconut leaves; that is life, and the mission is love. The purpose of the older living coconut leaf is to nurture coconut trees and give life to the delicious coconut. When you want to be loved, want to have children, and nourish the baby, then you see very clearly that you have love and have meaning in life. Our mission is to feed our children like the older coconut leaves nurtures the young ones. The deer or the lion also take care of their children with all their love. There are times when a mother lion fasts to save food for her children, because she has love, she has a meaning of life. We are nourished by a loving heart, a meaningful life, and then we discover ourselves, discover our loved ones, and we are able to love and give joy to others.

Then we will see life is meaningful, life is very mysterious, and we will cherish life. We must live and behave so that every moment of our daily life is able to nourish our love like coconut leaves; we protect our coconut leaves, grow the trunk, give delicious fruit to life. Therefore, you need to have mindful consciousness in order to feel life. Just walking on the ground with a conscious mind, a seeing and knowing mind, is already a miracle.

> *"Mindfulness not distracted*
> *With the shining brightness of wisdom*
> *Step by step on back the true home*
> *Life is a miracle."*

34

MINDFULNESS IS THE PURPOSE OF LIFE

"Life is really meaningful when we are awake or we have mindfulness because awareness is the source of happiness, mindfulness is the source of peace. This is the basic element to satisfy the goals of our life."

What is the purpose of life? This question is answered by older people for whom the purpose of life is to live a virtuous life. The virtue here is very beautiful and means that people live honestly, humbly, and with loving. When older people define life as such, it is because they have experienced the ups and downs of life, many triumphs and losses, success, glory and humiliation, only to return to one simple human life. Material life without spiritual life can cause suffering, tormenting the body and mind. The same question, when asked about someone who has just graduated, receives a different response: he starts a company that is doing well, and of course he does not agree with the retirees, because his purpose in life is to be a leader, and because he thinks life must be about material comforts and cannot be honest. In the market, too much honesty will not make money. Young people claim that life with less money is hard to live, because they cannot travel, their friends may stay away, and because money decides everything. Each answer has its own meaning. When an older person experiences life, they see that all material things in life do not make true happiness. On the contrary, young people who have strong vitality have not yet tasted life like the elderly, therefore the young ones do not see the importance of spiritual value.

The value of life is not on hold, waiting until old age; our life is pushed back and forth, bruised, and then we have a need to find the spiritual life. Also, young people spend a lot of time to have a career, make a lot of money, and it is not until they retire that they look for religion. In old age, we are not healthy enough to learn religion, so remember not to wait for tomorrow, because life might not have tomorrow. Life is really meaningful when we are awake or we have mindfulness because awareness is the source of happiness, mindfulness is the source of peace. This is the basic element to satisfy the goals of our lives. So, can we say here then that mindfulness should be put first because it will be a necessary precursor to all other goals.

The Pali word *Brahmacariya* means the observance of vows of holiness, particularly of chastity, and good and moral living. This life is meaningful, and we must have awareness to enjoy the best time when we are living. Be aware that human life is short, so do not waste time on the illusionary game of life. Having a negative, sad mind will detain you and you will remain in the midst of suffering and loneliness.

Do not have a headache because of anxiety. An evil mind can cause disease for our body. Sadness can cause food to be tasteless when we eat and can cause many nightmares. Lacking alertness causes us to be unable to take full advantage of our abilities and causes many negative reactions to our lives. I advise; do not let all the hardships cause you to think life is suffering. Why not forgive, since there is nothing unforgivable which we have suffered. Because life is a process of practice, hardships are an opportunity for you to learn and grow. You need to experience difficulties to have intellectual development. A negative mind is always hidden quietly inside us to destroy our happiness and peace, so watch negativity and do not allow it to harm your life. Awake and recognize. For example, when anger arises, then have the courage to face your emotion and say, "Hello! You are visiting me! I am here to face you!" Without recognizing anger, it can burn the wealth and career that we have built up throughout our life. An invisible emotion that bears in us, acts without control, seems crazy and loses the notion of the ability to discriminate, saying unreasonable things; that should not happen. When the anger decreases, we realize that we are bad, regret our faults, but it is too late because we already have created bad karma.

233
MINDFULNESS IS THE PURPOSE OF LIFE

When something goes wrong, we usually think the perpetrator is someone who has stood behind us to instigate, or has directly or indirectly provoked, or thought of hatred somewhere. We tend to look outside for condemnation and try to protect ourselves. But the outsider is not the greatest enemy, and if he loses his heart to someone, he also can become a close friend. This is because human nature desires to live peacefully and avoid suffering. If we think that the enemy is the one who causes us to become upset, makes us anxious and fearful, whether the harm only comes in the short or long term, then in our body is our culprit. If our life is lacking mindful awareness it will impact the body and mind when our body is sore, tired; when the sadness of anger makes us uncomfortable, frustrated, discouraged, and miserable. Mind defilement is an enemy. Anxiety, sadness, jealousy, anger, blame, doubt, and selfishness are our enemy. Negativity is a real foe, because it causes so many calamities and suffering for others. To be happy, liberated, you do not have to change this body, do not have to move to another planet. If living in heaven, but with an evil mind, then how can peace exist? There are people who get married and do not know how take care of themselves and their family and also are frustrated and bored, and some say, "I'm wandering alone in the world." If people do not have mindfulness, there is no guarantee for happiness, and it doesn't matter if they are married or not.

Living on happiness

In ancient times, the kings built many solid palaces to avoid war that endangered lives, such as The Great Wall of China or the many palaces in Rome and Greece that were built for that purpose. People lived in a safe and secure area, the soldiers guarded these places twenty-four hours a day, and no one was allowed in, even tiny animals. Just as many leaders were slain by traitors hiding within the depths of those secure areas, there are traitors that lies in you; greed, anger, and ignorance. Soldiers cannot see these enemies, and there is no panacea that can eradicate that type of affliction in you.

Even if we are enslaved by foreign invaders or a hostile world, they will not bring us to the extreme of suffering. The harm of internal suffering is more tragic than the suffering itself, as it silently harms and destroys our life. Any suffering brought by the outside will be gone someday and sometimes enemies become friends with each other. But the enemies that are ignorance, unawareness and lack of mindfulness cause perpetual suffering, and with these present you will never have true happiness. Using right understanding to see the source of our enemies within us, courageously confronting them to embrace and transform negativity is essential. Practicing mindfulness meditation is one of the methods for transforming defilements.

When confronted with a disagreement, the mind is sad, angry and cannot sleep. Often, we just try to take care of our body, but rarely awake to eliminate the affliction to achieve peace and happiness in life. If you have awareness and mindfulness, you have the opportunity to identify the mind of good and bad deeds. When an unwholesome idea arises, watching and being aware of it will lessen its fault. Paying attention to follow our thinking is essential in life. Your mind, like an elephant let roam around without the trainer, will be devastating and dangerous. When the mind is not mindful it will cause destructive power, which is stronger than all other types of destruction. The Buddha taught: "Mind is the forerunner of (all good). Mind is chief; mind-made are they. If one speaks or acts with pure mind, because of that, happiness follows one, even as one's shadow that never leaves" [61]

Mindfulness and awakening are the keys to nourishing the mind in purity and peacefulness. Being aware does not mean that you run away into the deep forest, hiding in the snowy mountains and not contact anyone. To be aware is to awaken to know what you are doing and what's going on around you. It is a state of knowledge of life, understanding of life. Then you will realize knowing life is sometimes painful, desperate, lonely and sad, but we still should find life interesting, meaningful, and worth living. Awakening is a miracle.

> *"To be mindful, Seeing clearly the object*
> *The afflictions are not affected and avoid suffering*
> *Achieve pure virtue*
> *Awakening the purpose of life."*

35

UNDERSTANDING MYSTERIOUS TRUTH

> *"Understanding the meaning of the four noble truths you see clearly that the attitude of honesty and transparence in real life, it is a deep understanding after experiencing and observing life. This attitude is not pessimistic or optimistic, negative or positive, but only perception and evaluation of life."*

The Pali word, *ariyasacca*, meaning verity of truth, means the teaching about the four Noble Truths. Why is this truth considering the most fundamental? Most important? And why are all Buddhist texts based on this truth? One truth in life is that everyone has a desire to stay away from suffering and seek happiness and peace. It is an inborn instinct of human existence. Peace is the desire of all of us, and of course that can be met. Suffering is a thing that everyone wants to get away from; if they try to attain sober awareness they will overcome all suffering. The purpose of human life is to seek happiness and avoid suffering, which is a very natural necessity. The Buddha was born with the purpose of pointing out the causes of suffering and teaching the way out of suffering in order to be happy and free. The problem is that you have to work hard to learn and practice to meet that desire. Four Noble Truths: (1) *Dukkha* - The truth of suffering; (2) *Samudaya* - The Truth of the Cause of Suffering; (3) *Nirodha* - The Truth of the End of Suffering; and (4) *Magga* - The Truth of the Path to the End of Suffering.

The Pali word, *dukkda,* means suffering, pain, and satisfactoriness. Suffering is a truth that you need to admit courageously, and you cannot pretend to ignore or to be not aware of it. If in life there are insecurities, no harmony among your family, no communication between your siblings and your parents, the atmosphere in the house is negatively affected, and you must courageously recognize it. An honest acceptance of the presence of pain is the first truth called the truth of suffering; recognition of suffering and knowledge about the suffering is a real thing. This view is very important, because there are those of us who are tormented without knowing the existence of suffering, so it is an unconscious confusion. When you can accept and recognize the suffering that exists in you, in your family, you begin to awaken.

The Buddha means an awakening person with perception, recognition, and understanding. An enlightened person is a person who is awake, aware of the painful nature of suffering. There is nothing special about suffering that is called the noble truth or holy truth. The reason that suffering is named a mysterious truth is because if you reflect deeply within suffering you will see the cause of suffering and find the truth of the path to the end of suffering, and that is the fourth noble truth. To go to the way of eliminating suffering, you must identify suffering in a comprehensive way.

The more you learn the meaning of the four noble truths, the more you see the true and clear attitude of honest life, which is a deep understanding after experiencing and carefully observing life. This attitude is not pessimistic or optimistic, negative or positive, but only perceiving and evaluating life. The attitude of life in Buddhism is not related to optimism or pessimism, or life avoidance. The Buddha advocated the middle way in terms of awareness and action through right speech, right action, right livelihood, right concentration, right mindfulness and right concentration.

Pain and the path out of suffering are very closely related to each other. Unconscious mindfulness never sees that the fourth truth is the way out of suffering. Therefore, avoiding suffering is the biggest mistake in life. It takes courage to name the suffering to understand the content of it. If you and your loved ones are angry at each other because of not having the same point of view, a lack of good communication, opposing each other, will lead to dissolution of family happiness.

Make yourself a doctor to diagnose the disease caused by the symptoms. This disease, called dukkha, caused by dissonance, anger, reproach, and division, is the truth of the cause of suffering. Root means the cause, the reason, the situation that occurs. When you know the causes of suffering then you will find ways to transform suffering, happiness will be present, and it will be the end of suffering. People tend to run away without courage to face suffering in order to transform it, as if they are not brave enough to face their true selves. When I feel lonely, have an empty heart, and a sad mind, I do not want to talk or communicate with anyone. People around me have abandoned me, do not associate with me, and do not care about me so I must find something fun to fill the emptiness. And you can go to the bar, enjoy all-night dining, or go to the casino, which is the normal way of current society. In daytime, suffering can be filled by this task, by being busy with the other task, but at night the pain is awake, your body is sleeping but your mind is not, and the nightmares are terrible. People are haunted by those nightmares all day long, feeling scared, and worried. Many people have fallen into deadlock and become depressed. It does not mean that they do not love their families or that they do not want to communicate with their siblings and loved ones. The truth is that they want to have a joyful family, but they cannot do so because there is too much unsolved pain in their hearts. Each person looks for their own amusement, holding an iPhone to chat with this person to fill the time; or opening an iPad to play games to fill the emptiness; watching emotional movies to pass time. At the airport, you only see people bending down to look at smart phones or electronic objects to play games or watch the news on Facebook. This running away contribution to the disease is a part of the times that has been happening to so many families.

Many people consider entertainment such as Facebook a tool for solving life's shortcomings as a civil aspect of modern society, but according to the Buddha, suffering is only solved when you know to look back to identify the cause and name it correctly in order to solve it in a religious way. It is very important to know the truth to identify the causes of suffering. Pain is never resolved by suppression or relieved by entertainment. If you can control the mind then the thoughts, the unprincipled actions, and the emotions will not disturb you anymore.

> "Comprehend Four Noble Truths thoroughly
> That the truth is mysterious
> Good enlightened teacher
> the end of all sufferings."

36

REALIZATION OF NIBBANA

"If you have the ability to come into contact with reality, live with mindfulness of awareness in your daily life, it is Nibbana."

Nibbana is a supreme peaceful status of liberation that practitioners aspire to attain. A joy acquired by the practice but that cannot be described in words. That view is somewhat correct, because there are things that need to be touched directly to feel them, only the practical experience can be felt. No matter how well your language is used, it is difficult to accurately describe what you have experienced. For example, if a person has never seen a coconut, has never had coconut water, and has never had coconut meat to eat, no matter how good your words are, it is difficult to give the other person an understanding of the good taste of the coconut.

In the Christian tradition, it is said that we are only able to experience God directly, and that we cannot discuss

God. But how do you do not talk about God, when there are many books written about Him and there are many institutes about God? At Western universities, there is a specialized study of God, called *theology*. Is this not a contradiction?

If you speak clearly to a person who has not had a chance to eat coconut and he listens to you closely, and the speaker does not set a net and the listener does not have eyes on the net, so neither of you are trapped, how can you use words to guide the other person to figure out the coconut? You say, Oh! You have not eaten coconut? Coconut skin is pretty hard, so after using the knife to remove the outer shell, you have to find the holes near the top and to get a stick to breach, pour water into the glass to drink, and then bang two coconuts against each other. They will burst; the meat inside the coconut is delicious. Coconut in Florida is the best in the United States. Although the other person has never eaten coconut, there was a clear enough description that he could find it and recognize the coconut.

Skillfully using language so the listeners are not confused can help you reach nibbana. In the sutras, all the Buddha's teachings are very meaningful, like the finger pointing to the moon. Although the finger is not the moon, the finger can point to the moon's position. When you want to see the moon, you need to look wisely; if your eyes look beyond your fingers then the moon is seen. Using ingenious means can help you to experience what cannot be said; expressing what cannot to be expressed in words is a talent.

It can be said that the ultimate goal of Buddhist practice is to reach nibbana. The word in *pali*, nibbana, means extinction, it means extinguishment, as the image of a fire is extinguished; it is the absence of ignorance and affliction. Nibbana is not an object but the nature of all objects. Nibbana can be contacted in this present moment, without escaping from this world and this life.

Theologians have said that you must have faith! If there is a heaven, if there is a God, you will be there. If not, then you lose nothing. If you do not believe that there is a perfect God, and there is a heavenly dreaming splendor, it would be so wasteful. All the effort and energy invested in a life without any belief is wasted when people ask whether nibbana exists or not.

In Buddhism, nibbana is either a reality or just an abstract idea of human imagination or exists because life is so miserable that people want to find a place where there is no more suffering. In Buddhist literature, nibbana means neither being nor nonbeing; it means that which is beyond being and nonbeing. If the definition of nibbana is being, then it would be wrong because the nature of nibbana goes beyond the notion of being; and saying nibbana is nonbeing is also wrong, because nibbana has no thought of nonbeing. The two concepts of "being and nonbeing" cannot be applied to nibbana. Nibbana is neither being nor nonbeing. You are an existing entity and nibbana also exists, meaning that an existence meets another existence. If nibbana is none, it would mean one has met no one, so wastefulness is a sure thing. The skepticism in the above-mentioned case relates to whether God and heaven exist in view of nibbana of Buddhist doctrine. Use the mind of the accountant to say, "be sure to have nibbana, then to play." If nibbaba has exhausted all effort only to miss nibbaba, then it is the biggest of losses. That is commercial thinking. Nibbana is the absence of the notion of yes and no, so requiring nibbana to be a yes would be a mistake from the beginning.

Paul Tillich, a German theologian, said that all that exists in the world, such as rivers, trees, rocks, animals, people, time, and space, belong to *being*. According to the doctrine of causality in Buddhism, the notion of existence can only arise from the notion of *non-being*. If there is no being, there would be no non-being, just as the notion of the right hand must be established with the notion of the left hand. If there is a right hand then there is a left hand. If we say that God is the foundation of existence, then who is the foundation of the non-existence?

Master Nāgārjuna, a great teacher in the Mahayana literature, defined, "Neither birth nor death, neither end nor permanence, neither identify nor difference, neither coming nor going, it is called *nibbana*." Nibbana means the extinguishment of all your notions of being but not extinguishments of nonbeing.

Perfect enlightenment means not that from going from having nothing to having. You do not have any chickens, now suddenly you have a chicken. The question is, where does the chicken come from? If the answer is "chickens come from hatching eggs!" we should ask, "who gave birth to the egg?" Saying the chicken is incorrect, and saying the egg is also wrong. The best answer is that no one comes first and from nowhere; that is called infinity or futility. From no coming, no going, we have reality.

Perfect enlightenment also means no defilement, no immaculacy, no increasing, no decreasing. The reality of nibbana is above all notions of defilement or immaculacy and increasing or decreasing. This concept has nothing to do with the truth. Going from a state in which ~~where~~ there is nothing to a state of existence to again nothing is called obtaining and forgoing. A lack of obtaining and forgoing is the characteristic of nibbana. This means neither annihilation nor permanence; annihilation is *non-being*; non-being cannot become being; permanence is being; the being is always the being. In reality, nibbana is beyond the notion of annihilation and permanence, defilement and immaculacy, increasing and decreasing. There is no birth and no death; birth is going from non-existence to existence; death is the notion of having nothing.

Therefore, it is very funny when you say nibbana exists or not. Nibbana goes beyond the reciprocal category end - permanence, identify - difference, coming - going, and birth - death. When you say nibbana exists then it is a mistake; if you say nibbana does not exist, it would be a bigger mistake. Therefore, the question, "If I am not sure if there is nibbana, then do I not want to lead a religious life?" Are these wrong words which sound very funny? With the idea of having - not having, in order to find nibbāna, you will never reach it.

Nibbana is a state of tranquility, called *the Ultimate Dimension*. Water is expressed in the high and low waves; sometimes they exist, sometimes not. The high and low waves, having the waves or not having waves is, in reality, water, and it is called *the Historical Dimension*. These waves have manifested the states of mind as anxiety, jealousy, suffering, fear; all these waves want to find happiness. Being and non-being are like waves and water. It sounds funny when we think that the waves are looking for the water because naturally waves are from the water. In the same way, nibbana is the essence inside you, which is neither birth nor death, neither end nor permanence, neither identity nor difference, neither coming nor going. You already have nibbana without searching for it. Is there nibbana or not? Or is there attainment or obtainment of nibbana? Both are very naive questions. As snow does not need to find water since the nature of the snow is water, this is called obtainment. The doctrine of the Buddha explains, nibbana is a state of avoiding of suffering, it is here and now.

A meditator went to the monastery and asked his Zen master: Dear Master, I am so distressed since I am an outcast, my parents are cruel to me, my wife abandoned me, my siblings betrayed me, my friends destroy me. What should I do to shake off this resentment and hatred?

The Zen master replied: "You sit down and concentrate, forgive them all!"

After a week of Koan practice, the practitioner returned to the monastery: I forgave them all. Lightly! Done!

Zen master said: Not yet! You need to be calm, open up and love them with your pure heart! The practitioner scratched his head and said: It is too hard to forgive them, now I have to love them then ..., then ...! Yes, I will try to do it.

After a week, the practitioner returned with a cheerful face, and happily reported to his Zen master that he already did love those who had previously treated him cruelly. The Master nodded and said: "Nice job! Now you go back, calm yourself and thank them. Without their roles, you do not have the opportunity to evolve spiritually. Salute them and give them."

The next time the practitioner returned, he believed that he finished his work. The disciple was happy to say that, Dear master! I have thanked everyone as it is because of them that I learned forgiveness, tolerance!

The teacher smiled and said: Then you go back to calm yourself again. These people have played their role properly, what mistakes did they make for you to forgive or not forgive?

The nature of holiness, the heart of tolerance, forgiveness, and abidance is inside each of us, thanks to the practice of mindfulness to brighten them. When you experience that you have a bodhichitta, a compassionate seed, a loving heart that understands, you are out of anxiety and fear. Just as the cloud knows that it is water itself, there is nothing to worry about. It is still fun and happy whether causing rain or snow. You have suffering, anxiety, and sadness due to the shadow of ignorance, which does not allow you to experience the depths of nibbana. If you become able to comprehend reality, living with mindfulness in your daily life, then it would be nibbana. Reality is the state of non-birth and not death, not dirty, not clean, not come, not go, not permanent, not breaking down, and through this all the sadness, despair, anxiety, and fear is gone. Everyone can do it, and everyone can attain nibbana.

The enlightened persons are those who walk on the earth with the life of being aware and mindful; therefore, wherever they are, they will be able to contact nibbana, and they will no longer waver with the loss, the competition, and the sadness of the world. Those persons have extinguished the afflictions, the ideas that are the identify - difference, birth-death, coming - going, being–nonbeing. When you are firm in the mind of these thoughts, you no longer suffer, and then you have true happiness, freedom and liberation.

> *"Understand the Buddha's teachings*
> *Practice the sacred path*
> *To achieve supreme peace*
> *And relation of nibbana."*

37

PEACE IS EVERY STEP

"If there is mindfulness then you live harmoniously, will not be bound, not be entangled by the loss or the gain of the world. The awakening mind is the key to developing profound spiritual qualities and beautiful fruits of peacefulness and happiness."

Life is a very abundant and diverse school, although there are no teachers, no lecture halls, no lesson plans, and it is without classrooms. But life gives you many precious lessons from the feeling of happiness and suffering, success and failure. When you are happy, it is a test given to you to see how emotional you are, how you take control of yourself when there is good news in your life; being happy with yourself could make you forget the compassionate virtue of humanity or not. Facing extreme suffering, do you keep calm in front of adversity? When you are down do you feel frustrated, depressed, anxious, scared and disappointed or not?

Grief's pouring down can make you lament fate: why is life so miserable, why was I treated heartlessly and with ingratitude like that?" It is a test to see if you are strong enough to stand up on your own feet after failure. When you succeed, it's a test of your humility in the light of glory. Could you proudly proclaim "Oh! I am a successful person in my life; nobody can be as good as I am!" Then you would be conceited, treating the people around you with arrogance and contempt.

All the states of mind, such as happiness and sadness are a test to see how mature you are, to see if you have courage and confidence in yourself, to see if you believe in this life which is often considered to be thankless. See if you are able not to lose your mind and love when you succeed, and do not be saddened by extreme suffering in the face of failure. If you have lost mindfulness, you cannot find your way; if there is no belief for you to rely on, then you are unable to believe in yourself, after being dealt misfortune in life.

In Pali, the word *Lokadhamma* means a motionless mind, not shaken when life or worldly blessings come. *Loka* means the world, but also means decay, disintegration, or destruction. The nature of the world always changes from one status to another, nothing is long lasting, even mountains and rivers change. *Lokadhamma* means the worldly dharmas; it means people often get caught up in the joyfull or sad status of life. The worldly dharmas have the eight kinds of wind: advantage (gain, prosperity or benefit), loss (decline), fame (honor), negativity (defamation), praise or laudation, blame (disparagement or ridicule), sorrow (suffering or dissatisfaction), and bliss (happiness, joy or pleasure). Among us there are many who are unable to face the ups and downs of life, have no faith in life after a failure, and have no confidence in themselves. The Buddha saw this as the cause of suffering, so He taught that it is important to stay in contact with the worldly dharma to maintain calmness.

The first perception is that your life has more difficulty, problems, and challenges than convenience, peace, and luck; even when making wrong and thoughtless decisions, leading to miserable actions, saying sordid words to others. You do not want this, but it has happened. Even so, you have a great deal of faith in life and believe in yourself, because there is something very interesting inside; there still are very nice people, and you can have an interesting life if you know how to live, to learn from failure. Life is a rehearsal which is like a game, but a serious game. Awaken to reflect on failures and difficulties in order to understand deeply and never to fall short and become depressed. Instead, find the best way to overcome and continue to practice this many times. Life is a long series of tests, which are certainly not repetitive, but the key to success is to look back to learn from useful experiences.

When faced with difficulty at work or when you're betrayed by your spouse, the first sentence you utter is likely to be: "Oh! my goodness! What is happening in my unlucky life? I did not commit any crime to bear such a misery!" Grievance, blaming this person, then blaming the other, blaming karma, or fate, condemning loved ones; that song is ringing through your ears continually, with a high loud voice throughout the day, and even at night it enters your sleep. The more you complain the more it proves that you have failed the test. Disappointment and difficulties in life are truly experiences that challenge your patience, your ability to let go, your forgiveness and wisdom.

There is a parable about a farmer's donkey falling into the deep abyss. The animal wept fiercely as the old man tried very hard to save his beloved animal from danger.

After many hours of trying only to fail, the old man decided that the donkey was old, and the abyss needed to be filled anyway. He called his neighbors to help him to fill that abyss.

Each man took the shovel, shoveled the soil and dropped it into the hole. At first, the donkey did not understand what was happening to him and cried more intensely. Then, to everyone's surprise, it began to silence.

After a few shovels, the old man looked down into the abyss and was surprised at what he saw. It turned out that after each shovel fell on his back, the donkey made an amazing start. He shook off the ground and stood up to the ground. As the neighbors continued to pour the land onto the animal's head, it continued to shake it off and stand on the soil. Soon everyone realized that the donkey had reached the mouth of the abyss and got out.

Life can pour everything on you, even the dirtiest things. The know-how is never to let it bury you. You can get out of the abyss by continuing to learn and never giving up. Then get rid of the hassle and move on.

We have the habit of reproaching and blaming those who have hurt us, blaming others who do not treat us well. Then we blame ourselves for being such foolish fools, naturally self-inflicting guilt on ourselves, not forgiving and self-tormenting; Oh! my goodness! Then people will know that we are fools. How can I put this face in front of the crowd! We must hide ourselves in another world!

This awkward thought means that there is no awareness of mindfulness in life, and selfishness, surrounds you. If you do not step out of the cycle of sadness and blame, then your life will forever be in slavery without freedom and serenity. The whole of life is a valuable lesson that you need to learn, because each failed or successful event contains worth to contemplate.

Someone asked, "What does life mean?" The answer depends on your level of maturity and readiness. Life can be ungrateful if you live irresponsibly, indifferent to people around you. On the contrary, if you have a noble attitude towards life and look at life with the eyes of love and duty, life is worth living. So, you never ask what life means. Ask how you see what this life means to you. Define for yourself a way of life, personal happiness, and your own values. Do whatever you think is meaningful, have fun in your life. Suffering or happiness depends on how you live your life. Beautiful ideals will motivate you to try out new things in life. One of these ideas is: I was born in this world to accomplish a life of worthwhile work, to learn lessons or to offer nice things to someone, to be responsible and fulfill my duty to myself, and other people. Looking at life that way then you can see everything is meaningful.

Maturity and stability are not dependent on age; there are older people who live without concept and their words of action are empty, and on the other hand there are young people who are really steadfast in a leisurely life thanks to the practice. Growing up with the firmness of the human being, regardless of age, has nothing to do with books, knowledge or others, but the experience of living with mindfulness in your daily life.

The human habit of dealing with a difficult problem is to try to escape, not to be brave enough to confront, not being calm enough to look at the cause, or to push it away for others to deal with. In this case you not only depend on your parents, your spouse, but also your children to solve your problems. If you rely on others, you will never grow up in life. Maturity is learned from failure; all hardships are meaningful and valuable lessons for you. When standing in front of the Buddha or Bodhisattva Avatars, you often pray for getting married to the one you love, to have a peaceful life, a family that lives in harmony, warmth in the quiet and good children. But you do not pray for yourself to have a strong will, hard-working faith to solve life's difficulties in a meaningful way to gain maturity.

Right view means that you have the right opinion about all matters, that you feel confident before every situation. Control your emotion; see how things are linked, what happens afterwards, whether it is beneficial or painful for others with your action. When you are in a state of alertness, whatever comes to your mind, whether happy or sad, you are ready to handle it in peace. In other words, when your mind is calm, relaxed, you can wander in a very free world. There are many people who ask what the Buddha is! There are many answers: "Buddhism is the way of wisdom." "Buddhism is the way of compassion." But I like to say, Buddhism is the religion of awareness. Because there is awareness of mindfulness, living is harmonious, not bound, entangled by the gain or the loss of the world. Mindfulness is the key to developing profound spiritual qualities and beautiful fruits that are in you.

> *"Mind is well static*
> *To living with Mindfulness and awakening*
> *Get rid of all ties*
> *Peace is every step."*

38

CALM AND JOYFUL MIND

"Be truly alert and diligent to practice; then you can see that the path of mind is abnormal and observe to know the nature of the mind's operation. Therefore, understanding of human nature in general and knowing the operation of the mind in particular is the most beneficial thing in the world."

The basic needs of humans are the physical necessities to maintain the body in daily life. Those undeniable requirements are to keep warm enough in winter and keep cool in the summer. Of course, recognizing the state of the mind, and mastering emotions while facing difficulties in life is the need that brings true happiness. Material deprivation is painful, when the necessities need to be met, but when the mind is bored, it is uncomfortable too. Sometimes when you want to find something in order to forget the sadness in your heart, you try to escape from it by doing things like watching a movie, watching television programs, etc ... although when you are finished watching the film you realize the boredom could not be solved. The reason is that your mind is still in the state of sadness from which has not been released. Instead of running away from boredom, if you know to come back to observe the mind, then you will see wakefulness, enlightenment and escape from the boredom.

The Buddha taught, be mindful to observe and care for your mind's garden so as not to be shaken. The word in Pali, *Asokaṃ,* means no resentment, no dryness, no sorrow, no sadness; it refers to a human being with freedom who could not be shaken by allowing sorrow to dominate.

Normally, your mind is always in a state of sleep. You need to act or stimulate the mind by doing things like reading, or listening to the doctrine by a spiritual teacher, so that your mind can wake up. Cultivate learning positive states so that the mind can nourish the good seed and heal the bad minds with rightful awareness in life. Similar to body care, you need lots of nutrients and many vitamins and minerals, not just having a few things but having variety. Likewise, caring for the mind involves many methods and solutions to increase the brightness of the mind, overcome the negative minds of continuous and complex change. In trying to change your shaking mind, your worrying mind and your uncontrollable emotion, you cannot succeed with just one or two methods. The change takes time and the practice is permanent. Even when you travel to another climate your body needs time to adapt. To maintain a clear, stable, and unsinkable mind is a process of learning.

Mental transformation is complex if there is no clear awareness and vice versa. There is great calm when the mind is trained and conditioned. The Buddha described the mind: "Hard to hold, to scare, follow the dancing sensuality; it is good to change the mind, ease the mind then peace comes." Everyone knows that people have minds that are hard to see and difficult to realize, but the mind plays an important role in your life. The shaking and distracted mind makes your life insecure, wildly crazy; with a mindful heart, you could have peace and happiness to reach a wonderful life. Because the mind is the center, it is the main object that plays an important role in the problem of human suffering or happiness; however, the mind is very difficult to see, is delicate, always panics, fluctuates, is difficult to hold, difficult to protect, difficult to recover, spinning along the labyrinth, constantly changing, jumping like a monkey climbing from branch to branch. The mind is important and difficult to grasp, so those who can control and master the mind are relaxed and peaceful.

If you are mindful of your awareness, know whether your mind is thinking about good or evil, knowing that about your mind is very important so that you can prevent bad thoughts from arising, while trying to train positive mind. Negative mind states include craving, anger, ignorance, jealousy, and conflict. These types of consciousness arise that make you fatigued, heavy, and cause many painful corollaries. On the contrary, nourishing kindness, such as love, understanding, tolerance, generosity, forgiveness, and charity, makes you pure and virtuous, making the experience of life free, peaceful, and meaningful. It is important to know how your mind is thinking, so that if the thoughts are good then you can maintain them and if they are unwholesome then you can give them up. Just by identifying and attempting to adjust the mind in that direction, you will have happiness and not fall into the path of suffering. The Buddha taught to nurture the mind:

Dear friend, with the purpose of making the unborn evil, unwholesome dharma, not to arise from the beginning, you should have the will to try to be diligent, mindful, and aware.

With the purpose of making the existing evil and the lawlessness to be eliminated, you should have the will to try to be diligent, mindful, and aware.

With the purpose of making the fruition of consciousness which has not yet been born to arise, you should have the will to try to be diligent, mindful, and aware.

With the purpose of making the existing fruition of consciousness possible to be maintained, not to be blinded, to be grown, to be generous, to be practiced, to be full, you should have the will to try to be diligent, mindful, and aware.

The mind is a complicated world, difficult to grasp, not easy to identify, operating under no law at all, and is very arbitrary and chaotic. As the vast and deep ocean contains many hidden potentials beneath, the surface is frequented by waves of hurricanes, such as fame, power, compliments, praise, and unfeeling. The sea of the mind is constantly pushing you to drift from east to west, from south to north, entangled in the matrix of the grid, blind and not knowing where the exit is. Be truly alert and diligent by looking to see the path of abnormality of the mind and use observation to know the nature of activity of the mind. Understanding human nature in general and understanding the operation of the mind in particular are the most beneficial things in the world.

The mind is the starting point, the gathering point, and peace is derived from the relaxed mind. If the mind is calm, everything is peaceful. In understanding the mind, all things are understood. The Buddha says, what is unwholesome, associated with unwholesomeness, belongs to unwholesomeness, all arises from the mind; whatever is good, is connected with good, belongs to good, all comes from the heart. From there, it gives us the assurance that suffering and psychological distress will be healed when human beings know to return to this very mind. It is only by changing the inside that there really is an outside change. Done this way, it is sometimes slow, but the result is a sure thing.

If you have a warm heart with love, forgiveness and great tolerance, or in other words, if you have a strong and clever inner self, all your outside troubles would gradually be resolved smoothly. The direct disorder of a community depends on and is guided by the self-inflicted disorder of the individual consciousness. That does not mean that humanity is doomed to remain in suffering, but it must wait until someday when the light of the dawn of all mankind is holy so it can be resolved. Vast history and experience shows that it takes only a few people with noble souls, courage and wisdom to create the locus of good, for with the attraction of the masses by the cause, hearts became generous and tolerant. However, sometimes you also see plenty of unwholesome power with many fascinating tricks to enchant people. But this leads to a tragic and humiliating result.

The mind needs to be protected and nourished by good basic qualities; there are always good seedlings; cleansed by the rain of love; cultivated by understanding ideas; that very mind becomes restless, and not be shaken by the winds of life because of strong inner will.

> *"The world is constantly moving*
> *Speech or intention*
> *To keep mind does not move*
> *Peace is follows"*

39

REMOVE AFFLICTION

"Suffering and afflictions are a fact of life, they are always with us and accompany us throughout our life. Do not run away from them, learn to let go of defilements into Bodhi, as suffering becomes peaceful as the gardener turns trash into flowers. And by adversity, you have the opportunity to grow up, which is the driving force to rise up in life."

Everyone wants to find happiness and shun suffering and distress in life. In fact, life always pushes us into the distressing circular defilements, and peace is rare as rain in a drought. If we just feel happy when the situation is calm, when there is no difficulty, and we are completely out of suffering, it is only a dream that can never exist in reality. Because the nature of life is full of obstacles and hardships, whether we want it or not we have to experience it. The concern here is how we can learn and practice to transform suffering into happiness, afflictions into bodhi, like gardeners who know how to make garbage into flowers.

Psychologists deal with defiled patients, people who must always turn their mind to something else, like blending a glass of lemonade with ice, listening to their favorite song, taking a break, thinking about funny stories, etc. The purpose is to distract their mind from the cause of affliction. It seems that the solution works temporarily and only evades. This method only suppresses that resentment and anger in their subconscious; it is still there, continuing to grow over time. On the surface, it seems like nothing. They can smile, communicate with people around them in a very normal way. However, in terms of subtle thoughts deep inside the mind, the volcano contains frustration, anger, discomfort, etc., sleeping and waiting for the opportunity to explode. Sooner or later these emotions will spurt in their actions, words, or thoughts. When these feelings are repressed they will not simply disappear but will become more intense than they were originally.

The Buddha expresses that *rajaṃ* means dust, indicating the affliction, and *vi* means get out. *Virajaṃ* means get out of afflictions. Afflictions are in one's mind which will make the mind obscene, as the dust makes the objects dirty, when we see the dirty things, we feel abhorrent, and do not want to touch them. If we must touch them we have to wash our dirty hands, but when the mind is cloudy, it makes the body more disgusting and there is no water that can clean it.

265
REMOVE AFFLICTION

Buddha's teachings tell us that, when confronted with defilements, first we must identify the suffering, find the cause of suffering, then propose ways to counter it, and carry out the process, then suffering will cease. This process is called the four noble truths. Thus, sorrows, anxieties, anger, conflict, and negativity are generated not only by the cause of the wrong perceptions but by many external forces. If you know how to stop bad seeds, happiness and peace will exist.

In our daily life, we only provide food to nourish the body, without caring for the mind, so we are always disturbed by mental torture. We do not pay attention to our mind therefore weeds grow all over the garden of the mind without letting us see flowers. If we do not know how to handle it, then flowers will not end up flowering and bearing fruit. A good gardener knows how to use weeds and garbage to fertilize the flowers. Instead of hating garbage, learn to love it more. In the same way, we must also face suffering and defilement. Therefore, you have to learn how to take care of the unwholesome mind in order to nourish the seed of the holy bodhichitta.

Another story is about a person who gets lost on a beautiful island, where the scenery is as stunning as in the land of elves. As soon as he entered the gate, someone dressed up elegantly greeted him and said: "You can enjoy everything you want, this place is full of food, full of entertainment, and around you have a lot of beautiful girls." He was so happy with experiencing the most comfortable living in the world that everyone always wants. He went from one great food to another, looked at the flowers in this place and walked around, and around him there was always a servant. Day after day, just enjoying life, he felt depressed and called for the servant.

"Is there anything here for me to do? I am very healthy if I keep eating and staying in the house, but I'm bored and I need something to do," he said.

The servant said, "Please, my dear that is the only request that we cannot satisfy. There is nothing here for you to do!"

"I'm really tired of this place; to be born in hell would be better than living here!" He said angrily.

The servant gently said, "So, where do you think this is?"

The story shows us, to achieve happiness, we must experience suffering, happiness cannot be in the absence of suffering; and if we want to achieve enlightenment we also have to understand defilements, because bodhichitta lies in the defilement. If we want to achieve a great career we need difficult experiences and afflictions. Studying and cultivating can never happen without suffering, afflictions, and distress. Without them we will not know peace, freedom, and the taste of liberation.

The practice of mindfulness meditation shows us that happiness is present when we know how to act and overcome suffering, observing that in suffering there is the root of happiness. In the bodhichitta there is the existence of defilement, in defilements there is existence of the bodhichitta. The important thing is our attitude when faced with afflictions or Bodhi.

Taking care of a child is a challenge, and we may feel we do not have enough compassion and patience to be a gentle mother, but we should be thankful and feel better than all things in this world, because we are truly glorified because this little angel has chosen us as his/her mother, he/she chooses to be our student and we are also the teacher of this child.

When our children grow up, sometimes they refuse to wear clothes that you choose for them, but do not take it as an act of disobedience, rather that our children are now old enough to choose for themselves. Our children are digging up the seeds that you planted in the garden, so instead of scolding them, you see that these are actions of curiosity, and they just want to find out how the seeds grow to become a tree.

Teaching our children is a great challenge, but never give up because this challenge has taught us how to live. Look at your children and you will see your ancestors being extended. And in life, if someone says bitter words to us, instead of condemning him to criticism, then you should think that he is a good person who has given us the opportunity to endure.

Living on happiness

Look at life with compassionate eyes, because with fresh friendliness, everything around us will become light and peaceful. Suffering and afflictions are inevitable; they are always with us and accompany us throughout our life. Do not run away from them, learn to let go of defilements and change them into Bodhi, because suffering becomes peaceful as a gardener turns garbage into a flower. And in adversity, we have the opportunity to grow up, as it is the driving force to raise ourselves up in life. Experiencing suffering, we will appreciate the true value of peace and happiness. Suffering is not always our enemy, and happiness and beauty are not always good for us. Life will not have any meaning in the absence of either suffering or happiness and finding our path to enlightenment and liberation will not be possible.

> *"Remove all troubles*
> *The insight often grows*
> *To realize our true nature*
> *Walking into the present moment."*

40

TOUCHING OF LIFE

"Happiness, peace, freedom, and pureness are in our mind. Just return to mindfulness, and strangely, we will discover many miracles of life. If we stop all thinking to contemplate, we can come into contact with these treasures now and here."

Life is a journey in which we are always busy with getting to know so many people, building a great career, and from that we think we have a rich diversity in life. But the most valuable thing is a sudden conception, in which we can find ourselves again, understand who we are, find our true selves. Then we realize that traveling all over the world will not equal finding the way back to ourselves or being in contact with life, which is a miracle and very mysterious.

If we live without knowing that we are alive, then our life is tasteless, worthless, and meaningless. The quote saying: "Living in drunkenness, dying in a dream" means that humans live without any ideal, with no meaning in life. There are many in today's society who have lived that way. So, we need to wake up to find out what we are doing, what are we eating, what are we drinking, who is reading, who is reasoning about psychology, who is just sitting there burning time with forgetfulness and carelessness. Being mindful is the beginning of consciousness, of finding the true life.

In Pali, the word *khemaṃ* means leisurely freedom. It is the human being who is able to come into contact with life, without fear, free from all accidents, overcoming obstacles, no longer busy, joyful, relaxed, beautiful and noble. In life we lose ourselves because of the grasp of circumstances, jobs, and habitat, so we are being distracted from returning, intact, to ourselves. Going back to our breath, mindfulness is present; that is, we can defeat the invaders of external circumstances and distraction.

When the light of consciousness is illuminated, the mind radiates, the door of freedom is revealed, the passage of the body of speech is also lit, autonomy is restored, the darkness of mindlessness no longer encroaches, the spiritual power is concentrated, nourished, and we become relaxed. Then in the day-to-day driving, mowing the lawn, eating rice, cleaning dishes, we become conscious and mindful in all movements, saying gentle words, and thinking clear thoughts. This is not something only for the beginners who come to the practice monastery, but even the great enlightened masters like the Buddha are still practicing. Mindfulness awakening and spiritual power are what characterize the great human beings.

Why use mindful thoughts in every gesture of our behavior? Because by virtue of mindfulness, we have the right view of the truth and recognize the existence of the reality of life. Stop thinking endlessly and bring back peace of mind. Keeping mind and body in mindfulness is essential to attaining insight, not the concept of sin or blessing while adhering to the precepts. There is righteousness, and there is morality. So do not cause suffering to anyone. When the scientist works in a laboratory, he does not eat, or drink, or listen to music, not because he thinks doing so is sinful. His reason is he is concerned that he will not give enough attention that he needs for his research. In the same way, Buddhist practices help us to stay in mindfulness in order to feel and be in touch with life.

Happiness is due to the inner calmness of the mind, and without inner peace, there is no peace outside. We have many conditions to help us be happy, but we do not know to cherish them. There is an unlucky man who is blind, who cannot see the beauty of nature. His dream is to have normal eyesight so he can see the sunset and the sunrise in the morning, which is to him it is the happiest feeling in the world. However, we all have bright eyes, but we do not know to cherish them.

272
Living on happiness

Practicing meditation helps us return to the present moment. If we do not have the ability to live in the present, or sacrifice the present to find a vague future, then we will bury our life. Learning Buddha's teachings helps us embraces life in the present, building a meaningful life, and ensuring a beautiful future. Setting up the best future is beginning to build a life that is profound in the present, responsible, loving, forgiving, and tolerant in life.

According to Buddha's teaching, happiness, peace, freedom, and pureness are in our mind. Strangely, just return to mindfulness, and we will discover many miracles in life. Know how to stop thinking and contemplating, and we can come into contact with these treasures now and here. A peaceful, happy life is a very important message of Buddhism, but this message gets very little interest to the public, seemingly forgotten and infatuated to a degree that amazes us. Exposing ourselves to the mysterious life of the present moment is easy according to the Buddha's teachings. Just returning to mindful breathing, words and actions, and thoughts is sufficient. Practicing these do not require us to go to the Buddhist monastery for sitting in the meditation hall, we can practice this method anytime and anywhere. Therefore, the Buddhists' teachings are lovely in the beginning, lovely in the middle, and lovely at the end. In practice, whether we are the beginner or long-time practitioner, there is happiness, the effect of peace and dharma.

Mindfulness is the heart of Buddhism. Basically, mindfulness is a very simple concept. The power of mindfulness is present when we practice and apply it to life. Mindfulness means to follow a special way, with a clear purpose, so that our mind can see what is going on without judging, to help us return to the present moment. Mindfulness will nurture a great sense of accepting reality. If we live without consciousness and are not fully in the present moment, we are not only missing out on the most precious inheritance in our life, but also cannot feel the precious treasure and the depth of opportunities that can help us grow and transform suffering. Mindfulness is also the way to help us master the direction and quality of life, including our relationships with family, society, and more to the world and the earth, and the root of bettering ourselves, as human beings.

> *"Exposure to life*
> *Mind often calm*
> *Does not release mindfulness*
> *Waking up the earth."*

41

HAPPINESS IN THE PRESENT MOMENT

"When your spirit is joyful, relaxed and you are loving life, everything around you become beautiful. The phenomenon of scenery happening around you is simple, natural and yet very wonderful and meaningful at the same time. Having peace of mind will help you to return to yourself, to feel the beauty of life and to appreciate the value of happiness."

A monastery gathered at the base of the mountain is a precious sight. Most monastics fully practice to have peacefulness and joy. One day they met to compile a list for supplies and to have one of the novices to go to the village to buy what was needed. The Venerable manager was very strict and stern with his instructions for the novice. "Buy only the items on the list and nothing else." The babe monk became very worried and fearful that he might forget something. He was not in the present moment. On his way to the village he was not paying attention to where he was walking. He missed a step on a rock and injured himself. When he got to the store he was in so much pain that he forgot what was on the list. He bought a few things, but not the right things. When he returned to the monastery to show what he had purchased, his manager was not happy. The Venerable Manager's scolding brought tears to the young monk's eyes as he was very sad and disappointed in himself. The novice's Master then consoled the babe monk and gave him new instructions. He said, "You go to village again and this time I want you to go with no fear and no worry. I want you to go slow, to be mindful of every step and observe everything that happens along the way and report it all back to me."

The novice knew of the warmth and love of the Master and could not say no to him. He went back to the village for the supplies, but this time he went in mindfulness. Not only was he able to buy all the right supplies, but his Venerable manager was so glad also. He also was able to notice all the beauty that surrounded him. He saw beautiful flowers and a murmuring stream. He heard the rhythm of eloquent bird song. He witnessed under a nearby tree a cute small doe grazing with his mother. As he was enjoying the beautiful scenery and the soulful freshness of the air, he looked up and saw his master smiling. As the Master sat waiting outside the entrance to the monastery, he witnessed the junior monk truly in the present moment. This made him very happy.

Living on happiness

The story of the novice's journey to buy supplies is a story of the journey of life. Life is full of interesting people and things. Life is a paradise where the soul can cultivate the values of love, peace, and happiness. Life can also be a constant misery if you don't know how to take care of the garden of your mind. Therefore, if you maintain your spiritual life you will know how to take care of your garden and you will have true happiness. If you can look at all the phenomenal things around you deeply and with loving eyes you will realize you have everything you need to be happy right now.

Throughout his 45 years' existence in the world, the Buddha traveled throughout India to teach about the path of transformation. Whether it was a short, medium, or long dharma talk, the intent was always to bring you back to your life in the present moment. He would use metaphors to teach love and understanding. He would invite you to live in the present moment so that you could experience happiness in life. There are thirty-eight dharma teachings in the sutras on how to live in the present moment. Each pathway in the teaching has a very deep meaning as it relates to life and when you apply them, happiness is present immediately.

Life always contains ups, downs, and adversity. Life also contains generosity, forgiveness, tolerance, and kindness. Daily life events have an impact on the soul to create a feeling of suffering or happiness. Each individual human being either experiences happiness or suffering depending on their acceptance of life events. Suffering, however, has an important role. Without ever having suffered we would not be able to recognize the feeling of happiness in our life.

The key to having true happiness in your life is being in the present moment and knowing what is going on around you. When you notice your mind is rushing, racing, and worrying about everything, then you know this is not the right mind to cultivate the value of happiness. Happiness is available when you truly return to the present moment. Experiencing a life where your soul is relaxed and well-rounded, gives you confidence, more vitality, and a beautiful direction in life. Pressures of life can be a heavy weight on your shoulders.

It can be said that when your spirit is joyful and relaxed and you are loving life, everything around you become beautiful. The phenomenon of scenery happening around you is simple and natural and yet very wonderful and extremely meaningful. When you return to the present moment you will feel the beauty of life and appreciate the value of happiness.

Therefore, the Pure Land or the heavenly realm, is right here, right now in this life. If your mind is clear, if you have the right view, if you are mindful with your words, actions, and thoughts, then you have the nucleus that brings happiness. Life feels valuable when you can recognize your adversities and transform your feelings.

Living on happiness

If you have suffered from cold and hunger, you will appreciate food and warm clothes. If you have suffered sickness, you will appreciate good health. When you experience the ups and downs of life in the moment you can show tolerance, gratitude, and generosity. If you have felt the pain of separation you will recognize the happiness of being with loved ones. Your difficulty and adversity become fertilizer for the seed of happiness. Thus, you are able to sympathize with and understand the pain of the people around you. Compassion and happiness can be present while at the same time you are facing the difficulties and adversities of life.

> *"While facing adversity,*
> *you can recognize your body and mind,*
> *can stay with peace,*
> *and find happiness in the present moment."*

DISCOURSE ON HAPPINESS[62]

I heard these words of the Buddha one time when the Lord was living in the vicinity of Savatthi at the Anathapindika Monastery in the Jeta Grove. Late at night, a deva appeared whose light and beauty made the whole Jeta Grove shine radiantly. After paying respects to the Buddha, the deva asked him a question in the form of a verse:

> "Many gods and men are eager to know
> what are the greatest blessings
> which bring about a peaceful and happy life.
> Please, Tathagata, will you teach us?"

(This is the Buddha's answer):

> "Not to be associated with the foolish ones,
> to live in the company of wise people,
> honoring those who are worth honoring –
> this is the greatest happiness.
>
> "To live in a good environment,
> to have planted good seeds,

and to realize that you are on the right path –
this is the greatest happiness.

"To have a chance to learn and grow,
to be skillful in your profession or craft,
practicing the precepts and loving speech –
this is the greatest happiness.

"To be able to serve and support your parents,
to cherish and love your family,
to have a vocation that brings you joy –
this is the greatest happiness.

"To live honestly, generous in giving,
to offer support to relatives and friends,
living a life of blameless conduct –
this is the greatest happiness.

"To avoid unwholesome actions,
not caught by alcoholism or drugs,
and to be diligent in doing good things –
this is the greatest happiness.

"To be humble and polite in manner,
to be grateful and content with a simple life,
not missing the occasion to learn the Dharma –
this is the greatest happiness.

"To persevere and be open to change,
to have regular contact with monks and nuns,
and to fully participate in Dharma discussions –
this is the greatest happiness.

"To live diligently and attentively,
to perceive the Noble Truths,
and to realize Nirvana –
this is the greatest happiness.

"To live in the world
with your heart undisturbed by the world,
with all sorrows ended, dwelling in peace –
this is the greatest happiness.

"For he or she who accomplishes this,
unvanquished wherever she goes,
always he is safe and happy –
Happiness lives within oneself."

ENDNOTES

1. Mahamangala Sutta, Sutta Nipata, 2.4.
2. Bhikkhu Nanamoli and Bhikkhu Boddhi, *The Middle Length Discourses of the Buddha*, 115- Bahudhatuka Sutta - *The Many Kinds of Elements*, Boston, 1995, p.927.
3. *The Book of the Kindred Saying*, Vol, 5. The Pali Text Society, London, Oxford, 2005. p. 172.
4. Ibid, p.172.
5. Ibid, p.219.
6. Ibid, p.172.
7. Translated from Pali name: Mahamangala Sutta, Sutta Nipata I.
8. *Khuddakapatha*, The Pali Text Society, 2005. p.3. "*Bahū devā manussā ca, Mangalāni acintayum, Ākankhamānā sotthānam, Brūhi mangalam uttamam.*"
9. K.Sri Dhammananda, *Buddhism in the Eyes of Intellectuals*, Buddhist Missionary Society, 1992, p.21
10. Nhat Hanh, Thich, *Plum Village Chanting and Recitation Book*, Parallax Press, Berkeley, California, 2000, p.90.
11. Bhikkhu Bodhi, *The Numerical Discourses of the Buddha, A Translation o f the Anguttara Nikaya*, Wisdom Publication, Boston, 2012. p. 107-8.
12. Eagleman, David, *The Brain – The Story of You*, New York, 2015, p.10.
13. *Dialogues of the Buddha*, Part III, The Pali Text Society, 2010. p. 177.
14. *The Book of Gradual Sayings*, Vol.2, The Pali Text Society, 2008, p.186.
15. *Dhammapada*, The Pali Text Society, 2003, p. 51. "*E'er intent on concentration, joyful in peace of letting go, mindful, wise, the perfect Buddhas, to even devas they are dear.*"– verse 181

ENDNOTES

16 *The Book of the Kindred Sayings*, Vol.5. The Pali Text Society, 2005, p. 3.
17 *Middle Length Sayings*, Vol 3, The Pali Text Society, 2013. p. 216.
18 *Samyutta Nikaya*, Vol, 2. *Puttamamsa*, p. 97. (*manosañcetanā tatiyā*)
19 *Chinese Buddhist Electronic Text Association (CBETA)*, T02, no. 99, p. 76, c24
20 See *The Middle Length Sayings*, Vol, 1. The Pali Text Society, 2007, p. 14.
21 *The Book of the Gradual Sayings*, The Pali Text Society, 2008, p. 58-9.
22 *Middle Length Sayings*, Vol 3, The Pali Text Society, 2013, p. 201.
23 Walshe, Maurice, *The Long Discourses of of the Buddha*, Wisdom Publications, Boston, 1995, p. 231-2.
24 *Middle Length Sayings*, Vol 3, The Pali Text Society, 2013, p. 199.
25 See Thich Nhat Hanh, *Opening the Heart of the Cosmos*, Parallax Press, California, 2003, p. 30.
26 Ibid, p. 30.
27 Ibid, p. 23.
28 Tolle, Eckhart, *Awakening to Your Life's Purpose*, Penguin Group, 2011, p. 11.
29 Bhikkhu Bodhi, *The Connected Discourses of the Buddha, A New Translation of the Samyutta Nikaya*, Wisdom Publication, Boston, 2000. p. 169.
30 Ibid. p. 829.
31 Ibid. p. 819.
32 K. Sri Dhammananda, *The Dhamamapada*, Sanana Abhiwurdhi Wardhana Society, 1992. p.142. Verse, 54-5.
33 Bhikkhu Náóamoli, *The Path of Purification (Visuddhimagga)*, Buddhist Publication Society, Sri Lanka. 2010, p.13.
34 P. V. Bapat & A. Hirakawa, *Shan-Chien-P'i-P'o-Sha*, tr. 77-78.
35 Bhikkhu Bodhi, *The Numerical Discourses of the Buddha, A Translation of the Anguttara Nikaya*, Wisdom Publication, Boston, 2012. p. 189-193
36 Ibid. p. 526.
37 Reeves Gene, *The Lotus Sutra*, Wisdom Publication, Somerville, MA, 2008, p. 379.

38 Thich Nhat Hanh, *Chanting from the Heart Book*, Vol 2., Blue Cliff Monastery, 2013, p. 113.

39 Bhikkhu Bodhi, *The Numerical Discourses of the Buddha, A Translation of the Anguttara Nikaya*, Wisdom Publication, Boston, 2012. P. 153.

40 Maurice Walshe, *The Long Discourses of the Buddha: A Translation of the Digha Nikaya*, To Sigilakaw - Advice to Lay People. Wisdom Publications, Somerville, Massachusetts. Sigalaka Sutta: 1995. p. 467.

41 Five hellish deeds: Parricide (killing one's father), matricide (killing one's mother), killing an arhat, shedding the blood of a Buddha (causing the Buddhas to bleed), and destroying of the harmony of the sangha (causing disturbance and disruption of harmony).

42 Arthur S. Reber and Emily S. Reber (2001), *The Penguin Dictionary of Psychology*, 3rd Edition, Penguin Reference, New Delhi, p.13.

43 Tolle, Eckhart, *Awakening to Your Life's Purpose*, Penguin Group, 2011, p. 64.

44 Bhikkhu Nanamoli and Bhikkhu Boddhi, *The Middle Length Discourses of the Buddha, Advice to Rahula at Ambalatthika*, Boston, 1995, p. 523.

45 Bhikkhu Nanamoli and Bhikkhu Boddhi, *The Middle Length Discourses of the Buddha, Advice to Rahula at Ambalatthika*, Boston, 1995, p. 524.

46 See Bhikkhu Nanamoli & Bhikkhu Bodhi, *The Middle Length Discourses of the Buddha - A New Translation of the Majjhima Nikaya, Maharahulovada Sutta: The Greater Discourse of Advice to Rahula*, Buddhist Publication Society, Sri Lanka, 1995. p. 527.

47 Thich Nhat Hanh, *Plum Village Chanting and Recitation Book*, Parallax Press, Berkeley, California, 2000, p.147-8.

48 *Khuddakapatha*, The Pali Text Society, 2005. p. 3.

49 Chinese Buddhist Electronic Text Association (CBETA), T08, no. 235, p. 749, a12.

50 Chinese Buddhist Electronic Text Association (CBETA), T25, no. 1509, p. 304, c7.

51 Chinese Buddhist Electronic Text Association (CBETA), T14, no. 475, p. 538, b4-5.

52 Bhikkhu Bodhi, *The Numerical Discourses of the Buddha, A Translation of the Anguttara Nikaya*, Wisdom Publication, Boston, 2012, p. 660-1.

ENDNOTES

53. Bhikkhu Nanamoli and Bhikkhu Boddhi, *The Middle Length Discourses of the Buddha, Advice to Rahula at Ambalatthika*, Boston, 1995, p. 234.
54. Thich Nhat Hanh, *Plum Village Chanting and Recitation Book*, Berkeley, California, 2000, p. 229.
55. Nhat Hanh, Thich, *For A Future To Be Possible*, Berkeley, California, 1998, p. 62.
56. Thich Nhat Hanh, *Plum Village Chanting and Recitation Book*, Berkeley, California, 2000, p.21. (The five contemplations: (1) This food is a gift of the earth, the sky, numerous living beings, and much hard and loving work. (2) May we eat with mindfulness and gratitude so as to be worthy to receive this food. (3) May we recognize and transform unwholesome mental formations, especially our greed and learn to eat with moderation. (4) May we keep our compassion alive by eating in such a way that reduces the suffering of living beings, stops contributing to climate change, and heals and preserves our precious planet. (5) We accept this food so that we may nurture our brotherhood and sisterhood, build our Sangha, and nourish our ideal of serving all living beings).
57. Bhikkhu Nanamoli and Bhikkhu Bodhi, *The Middle Length Discourses of the Buddha; Vtakkasanthàna sutta, The Removal of Distracing Thoughts*. Boston, 1995. p.211.
58. Thich Nhat Hanh, *Chanting from the Heart*, Berkely, California, 2007, p. 318.
59. Thich Nhat Hanh, *The Other Shore*, Palm Leaves, Berkeley, California, 2017, p. 23.
60. Bhikkhu Nanamoli and Bhikkhu Boddhi, *The Middle Length Discourses of the Buddha, Advice to Punna*, Boston, 1995, p. 1118-9.
61. K. Sri Dhammananda, *The Dhamamapada*, Sanana Abhiwurdhi Wardhana Society, 1992. p.42.
62. *Mahamangala Sutta. Sutta Nipata 2.4,* From Thich Nhat Hanh, *Plum Village Chanting and Recitation Book*, Parallax Press, Berkeley, California, 2000, p. 230.

Vung Q Doan aka Minh Hai, graduated with a Bachelor in Buddhist Psychology Studies and with a Bachelor of Psychology. He is a translator, scholar, and currently a second-year student in the Educational Psychology M.A program. He has practiced mindful meditation and has been an avid follower of the traditional Zen Master Thich Nhat Hanh, since 2003. He also teaches to guide local youths in how to practice mindfulness in daily life and wants to brings to light the power meditation to achieve a happy life through mindful awareness, a practice that can be applied by anyone, anywhere.